Conserve the Converts

To

Ralph and Bernice and Peter
who followed me up

and to a corps of students from
Nazarene Theological Seminary who
have already demonstrated their
dedication to follow-up

CONSERVE THE CONVERTS

A MANUAL TO HELP PASTORS AND LAITY
CONSERVE THE RESULTS OF PERSONAL AND MASS EVANGELISM

BY
CHARLES "CHIC" SHAVER

Beacon Hill Press of Kansas City
Kansas City, Missouri

15   14   13   12   11   10   9

Contents

Preface		9
Definitions		11
Chapter 1	What's Happening at the Back Door?	13
Chapter 2	The First Four Steps in Follow-up	24
Chapter 3	What Do Babies Need?	35
Chapter 4	The Adventure of a Follow-up Call	48
Chapter 5	Equipping Saints for Follow-up	59
Chapter 6	Beyond *Basic Bible Studies*	68
Appendix A		77
Appendix B		87
Notes		101

Preface

MY PRAYER IS THAT THIS BOOK WILL BECOME the means of equipping established Christians to follow up new Christians until they, too, are established.

Since so many events in this book were witnessed by me personally, I have chosen to write in a natural style, using the first person pronoun freely. It just didn't seem right to describe my involvement in someone's spiritual birth by writing, "This author . . ."

Many of the references to local church settings name the Church of the Nazarene, where these events occurred. This book is written as a training text for the Nazarene denomination. However, I do hope that my Christian brothers and sisters in other denominations will find it useful in their churches as well. Follow-up is something we all need to do.

This book ought to be read with *Basic Bible Studies for New/Growing Christians* as a constant companion. How the two go together will be apparent as you read.

Special thanks should go to Paul Lorenzen, who has had a "parent heart" since I first knew him as a student. As a layman, associate pastor, and pastor, he has followed up converts. He is responsible for most of the Appendix B instructions for the use of *Basic Bible Studies,* and he developed much of the record system given in Appendix A. Further, I have drawn extensively on the series of articles on follow-up that he wrote for the *Preacher's Magazine.*

—CHARLES "CHIC" SHAVER

Definitions

CERTAIN TERMS WILL BE USED repeatedly in this book. It is best to become acquainted with the meaning of them now.

1. *Follow-up*—"the process of training and bringing spiritual children to a place of mature fellowship with Christ and service in the church."[1]

2. *"Basic Bible Studies for New/Growing Christians"* —a series of basic scriptural studies, to be used by a mature Christian to help establish a new Christian in his or her faith.

3. *Spiritual Parent*—the one most responsible, on the human level, for the spiritual birth of a Christian.

4. *Adoptive Spiritual Parent*—one who, though not responsible for the birth of a new Christian, agrees to take responsibility for his or her spiritual nurture. The spiritual parent adopts the spiritual child.

5. *Spiritual Birth Certificate*—a written statement indicating the time and date of spiritual birth for a new Christian.

6. *Mature Christian*—a Christian who has grown sufficiently to stand alone under temptation, is able to reproduce spiritually, is involved in service for Christ, and is responsibly related to a local church.

CHAPTER 1

What's Happening at the Back Door?

THE PASTOR AND I CALLED ON RON.[1] We had hoped to share Christ with him. Somehow he knew we were coming and sensed the purpose of our call, so he took his dog on an extended walk. We had a nice visit with his wife. It was easier for us to wait in the warmth inside the home than it was for Ron to walk his dog in the cold outside. Finally Ron came home.

It wasn't hard to talk to Ron after all. The conversation finally led to spiritual things. Ron and his wife were quite open to the gospel. The next morning was Sunday, and this couple was at church. When the invitation to receive Christ was given, they came forward, prayed, and made clear-cut statements to the fact that they had received Christ as their Savior. That evening the week of special services came to a close—and Ron and his wife were there. Ron vigorously shook my hand, thanked me for being concerned about him, and testified that Christ had already made a difference in their marriage. All the while he talked, his face was glowing. I'm convinced that Ron and his wife were truly converted, truly born again that weekend.

Since I was an evangelist, on Monday I left for my next meeting. But a few months later I saw that pastor again. I asked about Ron. Then I heard a sad story. For several weeks Ron had been a different person—coming to church, getting along with his wife, experiencing victory over alcohol, rejoicing in Christ. Then his interest seemed to lag a little.

The guys at work had discovered Ron was a Christian. One day a so-called buddy dialed the special phone number by which you could hear a recorded prayer. It's called "Dial-a-

13

Prayer." Just as the recording was about to start, he hollered, "Hey, Ron. It's a phone call for you. Someone from your church." When Ron answered the phone, he simply heard a strange voice praying for him. The guys just stood around and laughed. After that Ron didn't come to church much—he just fell away.

The Record of Losses

What a sad story! But it is not an exceptional one. All of us who have been in Christian work have seen persons who, like Ron, started out for Christ but who did not finish the race. A deadly attrition occurs because, as Paul warned the Ephesians, there are evil forces at work that try "to draw away the disciples" (Acts 20:30, NASB). Is there an almost mathematical equation that says, "If the pressure of the world is not equaled by the support of the Christians, the convert will be lost"?

The evidence of such losses mounts up. When I first began studying this issue, C. E. Autrey was reporting that shortcuts in conservation were costing Southern Baptists 200,000 converts annually.[2] A. C. Archibald stated, "A study of statistics from all major denominations for the past twenty years reveals that nearly 40% of our evangelistic recruits are lost to the church within seven years."[3]

In the Church of the Nazarene, in the 32 years prior to 1975, 728,967 members were received by profession of faith. During that same period, 395,828 members were removed or dismissed from membership or transferred to other denominations. That is a loss of over 54 percent.[4] While new people are being reached for Christ and coming into the church by the front door, a number equivalent to over one-half of them have been going out the back door.

The office of the general secretary of the Church of the Nazarene reports 152,914 new Nazarenes gained during the four years of 1976-79. During the same period, 70,121 were dismissed from membership or transferred to other denominations, a loss close to 46 percent. In the five years of 1980-84, new Nazarenes were 231,767 with 97,667 lost, or 42 percent.

In the quadrennium beginning 1993 and ending 1996, the church gained 338,051 new Nazarenes. In that same time frame, 142,563 were removed, released from membership, or transferred to other denominations—once again a 42 percent loss. It is hoped that this improvement in cutting losses may be attributed to increased concern for conserving and discipling converts, but 42 percent is still unacceptable.

The establishment of new converts to Christ is not an issue to be considered only for the church that has been lacking in love or zeal. A pastor of an aggressive, loving, zealous Florida Church of the Nazarene reports a growth of 100 to 150 a Sunday over last year's attendance. In the previous year 39 were received into membership by profession of faith. In the present year, from September through mid-December, this church has seen 45 people come to Christ in their homes. Yet this pastor affirms that an increased follow-up ministry is their church's biggest need.

A questionnaire on follow-up procedures used by local churches was sent to about 200 pastors several years ago. Most were pastors of Nazarene churches, and all were pastors of Evangelical churches. There were 110 responses received. They revealed that though 101 pastors personally followed up their converts and over 70 involved laymen in the visitation of these new believers, only 36 had any Bible study program in the home for these baby Christians. Fewer still, only 16 had an adoption or undershepherd program, by which established Christians were assigned to work with the new converts on a regular basis.

Follow-up Is Biblical

The history of the Early Church, as recorded in the Book of Acts, is filled with instruction and example of the concerned follow-up of converts. In Acts there are at least 32 follow-up instances and 18 occasions where the related concept of encouragement is displayed. Paul's follow-up practice is given in 14:21-22: "They preached the good news in that city and won a large number of disciples. Then they *returned* to Lystra, Iconium and Antioch, *strengthening* the disciples and encouraging them to *remain true* to the faith. 'We must go through many hardships to enter the kingdom of God,' they said" (italics mine).

In Paul's own early Christian life, follow-up by a loving Christian brother was a key factor in his establishment in the faith. Acts 9:26-27 records what I call "Paul's most dangerous moment." Paul had been converted, filled with the Spirit, baptized, and had preached his first sermons at Damascus (vv. 1-25). Then he sought the fellowship of the believers at Jerusalem. Due to his past persecution of their number, they were hesitant to accept him. So what happened? The *New English Bible* puts it this way: "When he reached Jerusalem he tried to join the body of disciples there; but they were all afraid of him, because they did not believe that he was really a convert. Barnabas, however, took him by the hand and introduced him to the apostles. He described to them how Saul had seen the Lord on his journey, and heard his voice, and how he had spoken out boldly in the name of Jesus at Damascus." Barnabas became Paul's friend, stayed close to him, introduced him to the Jerusalem brothers, and paved the way for his establishment in the fellowship. As a matter of fact, Barnabas was so good at this sort of thing that he was called the "Son of Encouragement" (4:36, NASB).

But you may wonder if we really need to be so concerned about following up new converts. After all, doesn't God have responsibility for their care? The Scriptures do say, "Being confident of this, that he who began a good work in you will carry it on to completion until the day of Christ Jesus" (Phil. 1:6). But, remember, those words of confidence are expressed by a Paul who exclaimed in the verses just previous: "I thank my God every time I remember you. In all my prayers for all of you, I always pray with joy" (vv. 3-4); and he followed his confidence of verse 6 by stating, "It is right for me to feel this way about all of you, since I have you in my heart" (v. 7).[5]

The man who has confidence in God's establishing a new convert is the same man who carries on a ministry of prayer for those converts and so identifies with them that he carries them in his heart. Our planned follow-up of a young Christian is not a minimizing of God's grace but a cooperation with that grace.

Even if 1 in 100 wandered away, Jesus Christ was not satisfied (Luke 15:3-7). The word to the spiritual leaders of the Ephesian church concerning their flock was "The Holy Spirit has made you overseers," not that they were to make God Overseer (Acts 20:28).

Present-Day Follow-up

Thus to face the problem of back-door losses and to be true to the scriptural teachings on concern for the convert, we must follow up our new Christians in a careful way. Paul Lorenzen has asked us to visualize a total evangelistic approach to a person on a scale running from 0 to 100. The different phases would look something like this:

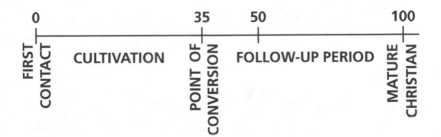

Lorenzen continues: "Evangelism which is properly done will include: (1) a proper amount of cultivation, (2) the point of conversion, and (3) a thorough period of follow-up with the convert. Any evangelism which does not include the follow-up in some manner is incomplete evangelism."[6]

Walter Henrichsen of the Navigators says that follow-up "deals with the development of new babes in Christ from the time of their new birth until they grow and provide for themselves."[7]

Dawson Trotman feels it may take from 20 weeks to two years to adequately strengthen a new convert.[8] Certainly the first year of a spiritual baby's life is an especially crucial time.

Can you remember when you were a new Christian? There were some things you didn't want to face alone. How many times it happened for me—as I was struggling over issues facing me in my new Christian life at a secular college. There would be a knock on the door, and my pastor and wife, Ralph and Bernice Ferrioli, would be ready to take me on a picnic, to come by and talk, to pray, to leave me a promise from the Word. Before we were using the term *follow-up* much in the church world, they were following me up. The 26 miles they drove from their little home mission church to my dorm, or the expense incurred in having me in their home for dinner over 40 times in two years, never seemed to phase them. They loved me and guided me in my first faltering steps for Christ.

The question is sometimes asked, "What percentage of our converts will be kept if we implement a follow-up program in our church?" I hesitate to suggest an exact percentage. One pastor testifies to about 75 percent assimilation of converts in two different churches where he directed the follow-up ministry.[9] The best way to answer the question is to say that in proportion to the increase in your loving follow-up efforts, you will witness increase in the stability of your converts. However, most follow-up efforts will not just occur automatically. You will need to plan for follow-up to happen in your local church.

Enough Love to Keep Them Warm

Not only is a plan for follow-up needed, but the whole atmosphere of the local church must be sympathetic to the nurture of young believers. Evangelist Modie Schoonover helped me see this. He said that if the church he pastored went a long time without winning any new people to Christ, he did not blame the sinners. Instead Schoonover would ask, "Has my church got enough love to keep them warm?"

A "church [with] enough love to keep them warm" —what did he mean? Well, such a church is like the hospital nursery. The newborn babies are not sent home three minutes after their birth to fend for themselves. Because of their fragile condition, they are put in a special place called a nursery. Here they receive warmth, love, and a special diet. In a germ-free atmosphere, they are cared for around the clock by specially trained nurses.

Likewise, in the spiritual realm, it is not enough for people to be born again, to be born spiritually. There must be a warm and loving spiritual atmosphere. There must be believers who will care for, feed, protect, and guide these new-born spiritual children during their first crucial days.

The excitement and joy at their child's birth would soon vanish if parents knew that in four days their child would die because no one would feed him or her! Does it bring glory to God to have new people converted to Christ at our altars or in their homes if it is also known that in a few days they would all die due to lack of spiritual care? If, for example, God were to give your church five brand-new adult converts within seven days, would your church have enough love to keep them warm?

That warm and loving church from another day is described in Acts 2:42-47 (NEB):

They met constantly to hear the apostles teach, and to share the common life, to break bread, and to pray. A sense of awe was everywhere, and many marvels and signs were brought about through the apostles. All whose faith had drawn them together held everything in common: they would sell their property and possessions and make a general distribution as the need of each required. With one mind they kept up their daily attendance at the temple, and, breaking bread in private houses, shared their meals with unaffected joy, as they praised God and enjoyed the favour of the whole people. And day by day the Lord added to their number those whom he was saving.

Don and Jane found a church with enough love to keep them warm. Don had been raised in a Nazarene pastor's home. Sometimes it happens—I don't know that I can tell you why—but Don rebelled against God and the church. At 12 he was smoking and at 16 was harsh and bitter. When he married Jane, he spoke critically to her of the Church of the Nazarene.

While Don was in the armed services, he received word that his mom was sick. He asked Jane to go north and visit her. After Jane had lived in the home of Don's parents for a few days, she realized there was genuine love there. Don's mother must have intentionally delayed her admission to the hospital until after Sunday. So Jane went to church with Don's parents. And what do you suppose happened? That Sunday Jane found the Lord.

When she returned to Don, he was not happy with the news of her conversion—especially since it happened in a Nazarene church. Shortly after her return, Don completed his stint in the service. They moved to a large Midwestern city. Not long after this move Jane became ill. The doctor told her she was suffering from a large cyst on a vital organ. Surgery was prescribed.

Jane confessed her concern about her physical condition and told Don she would feel much better about it if she could phone his folks. When one of Don's parents assured her over the phone, "Don't worry, Jane. We'll pray for you," she was sure that everything would be all right. Can you imagine the amazement of the surgeon when his examination just before the operation showed the cyst was gone? Apparently the Great Physician got there just before he did.

As Jane rejoiced over her restored health to her husband at home, Don responded, "Oh, Jane, I don't know why I've been so bitter. I know it's because of God and the prayers of Christians that you were healed." In the light of God's goodness, Don determined to change his attitude. He decided that he and Jane ought to go to church together the next Sunday.

So a struggling new Christian, Jane, and a formerly belligerent and now-beginning-to-soften Don went to church the next Sunday. Since Don had been raised in a Nazarene home, the couple chose to attend a Nazarene church. However, few at the church bothered to shake the visitors' hands. Apparently no one sat beside them in the pew. There was no invitation to dinner. No layperson from the church visited in their home that week or called them on the phone.

Don urged Jane not to be discouraged—they would go to another Nazarene church next week where the people would be friendly. But at the second church the same thing happened. Few greeted them, no one sat with them, there were no dinner invitations, no visitors came during the week. They went expecting a warm heart and only got a cold shoulder.

Before the third Sunday rolled around, a friend of Don's recommended a Church of the Nazarene known for its love. The men of that congregation have been known to stand in line to greet visitors. A lay couple of that church have the goal of either inviting each new couple into their home for dinner or visiting the couple within a week after their first attendance. Immediately Don and Jane felt the warmth of this fellowship. Don grinned at Jane, saying, "We've found our church."

On Monday the pastor left for district assembly and wasn't back until Thursday night; but Friday he called on Don and Jane. Don welcomed him on the doorstep and told him his laymen were "on the ball." A couple had already been there to visit them.

Sunday morning, Don and Jane were back in that Nazarene church. When the invitation to accept Christ was extended, Don headed down the aisle, arms swinging, and at the front knelt to pray. The pastor leaned over and asked him if the Lord had forgiven him. Don looked up, tears staining his handsome, rugged face: "I had to ask only once, Pastor!" The next day Don phoned his dad long-distance: "Dad, yesterday I met a lifelong friend of yours." His father replied, "Who was it, Son?" Don exclaimed, "It was the Lord Jesus Christ!"

Next Sunday Don and Jane knelt at the altar again, to find God's sanctifying power. The following Sunday they joined the church. The next week they had a part in pointing their first souls to Christ. Their church had special services nightly. Don and Jane attended every night but one, when Don's business took him away.

The closing day of the meeting a young engineer and his wife were in attendance. The wife came forward to pray. The husband was shy; he held back. But when the service was over, Don and Jane were at the back talking to the new couple. Don was inviting them to get together that week. How amazing! A few weeks before, Don and Jane had been looking for a church with enough love to keep them warm. Now they not only had found it but also were part of it.

The real test of our evangelistic effectiveness must ever be not how many are born, but how many are still living. Warm hearts and careful follow-up can narrow those back-door losses.

Questions for Discussion

1. Why is it imperative to follow up new converts?

2. What are the major sources of discouragement for the new Christian?

3. Why was Barnabas called the "Son of Encouragement"?

4. If there was a Barnabas in your early Christian life, share your experience with the class.

5. How would you answer the question "What percentage of our converts will be kept if we implement a follow-up program in our church?"

6. What is meant by the phrase "a church with enough love to keep them warm"?

7. What are some of the things we might do to show loving concern for the new converts?

8. What is the ultimate test of our evangelistic effectiveness?

CHAPTER 2

The First Four Steps in Follow-up

THAT FEBRUARY 13 WAS NO UNLUCKY DAY to my way of thinking. Tom and Laura had gone calling with me that Thursday night. We had an appointment with Fred and Patty Tucker and were graciously received. After talking about Fred's watch repair work and Patty's home and their son, Brad, we talked about their church backgrounds. Fred was a Catholic; and Patty, in her words, was "a nothing." They had been impressed by their visit the previous Sunday at the First Church of the Nazarene. So it was easy to begin discussing the central message of the Church—"that you may know that you have eternal life" (1 John 5:13).

Assurance from the Word

Until 11 P.M. we shared the gospel with them. Finally, they both wanted to pray and receive Christ. After prayer, Patty was brushing away tears, and Fred was serious and reverent. While the atmosphere was still reverent, I questioned Fred concerning the promise of Rev. 3:20, on which we'd based our prayer. "Fred, did you mean it when you told God you were sorry for your sins?"[1]

"Yes, I did," he responded.

I continued, "And did you mean it when you told Him you were opening the door of your heart?"

"Yes, sir!"

"Did Christ mean it when He said, 'If anyone hears my voice and opens the door, I will come in'?"

"He sure did!"

"Then," I asked, "where is Jesus Christ right now, Fred?"

A big smile—"Why, He's in my heart!"

"Are you just telling me that, or do you really know it?"

Fred beamed. "I know it."

I questioned Patty the same way. There were more tears and a positive response.

I turned in my New Testament to John 6:47. I showed it to Fred and Patty, and we read it together: "I tell you the truth, he who believes has everlasting life." Then I said something like this: "Fred, in the beginning you told me that you didn't know for sure you'd go to heaven, but you've prayed and asked Christ into your heart, and you told me that He's just come into your heart. Now, if anything should happen to you when you go to bed tonight and you should die in your sleep, where would you wake up in the morning?"

With a glow on his face, he said to me, "In heaven."

And I said, "Fred, welcome into the kingdom of God."

Patty was equally positive. A verse of assurance had strengthened their faith.

A Spiritual Birth Certificate

During my explanation of the gospel, especially the meaning of Rev. 3:20, I had shown Fred and Patty the pocket-size reproduction of Warner Sallman's famous painting of Christ knocking at the door of the heart.[2] I expressed my desire to leave that picture with them as a remembrance of the events of the evening. But first I turned the picture over and wrote on the back of it like this:

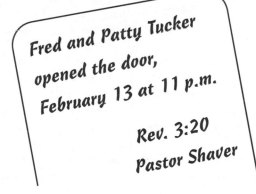

Fred and Patty Tucker
opened the door,
February 13 at 11 p.m.

Rev. 3:20
Pastor Shaver

I passed the picture to Fred and Patty to sign, for they were the ones to whom it had happened. I handed the picture to Tom and Laura, my calling partners, for them to sign; for they, as I, had seen all this happen. Upon presenting the picture to the Tuckers, I said, "There may be times when the devil will try to tell you nothing has happened to you, or your emotions may not be as strong as they are just now, but this picture will serve as a reminder of what Jesus Christ did at eleven o'clock this evening." This picture, filled out on the back, is called a Spiritual Birth Certificate.

Public Profession

I regularly urge new Christians to tell someone within 24 hours what Christ has done for them. In addition, I always ask them to make a public profession in church.

So I proceeded with Fred and Patty in this vein:

Here in the privacy of your home you have made a very important decision. You have received Christ into your heart. However, it is also important for you to go on public record and let others know about this decision. Jesus said that if we would confess Him before men, He would confess us before the Father (Matt. 10:32). I'm not sure you noticed last Sunday when you were in the worship service, but we have a place at the front of the sanctuary where people can kneel to pray. It's called an altar. Sometimes people go to the altar to pray to receive Christ, much as you have tonight. Other times Christians may go to the altar to pray about problems. Fred and Patty, you know there's another reason to go to the altar, and it is the fact that some people who have accepted Christ in their homes go forward in church as a public testimony that they have accepted Christ. Would you be willing in Sunday morning's service to go forward and kneel at the altar as a public testimony—"Yes, I have accepted Jesus Christ"? Would you promise God and me that you'd do that?[3]

The Tuckers readily promised that they would make a public profession of their new faith in Christ by going to the altar the next Sunday morning. We have discovered that getting the convert into the first Sunday's service and making public profession in that service is a high-priority item. Those who do not do so do not seem to do as well in continuing spiritual life as those who do. One reason the convert is asked to promise God he or she will make that public profession is to make it a truly serious thing with him or her.

A Promise to Do Bible Study

Next I asked Fred and Patty to think about their son, Brad, for a minute. Brad was about two years old, had been on the scene all the time we had been sharing the gospel, and had been extremely well behaved. I questioned, "Do you remember when Brad was born? That was a big day in your lives. But what if you'd never fed him after he'd been born?"

Fred answered, "He would have gotten sick and died."

I responded: "And the same is true spiritually. Tonight you have been born spiritually. The Bible calls it being 'born again.' But it is important for you to take in spiritual food to keep alive and keep growing. One way a Christian grows is to read the Word of God, along with other things. Now I have a little Bible study here that I usually carry with me. I wonder if you would be willing to do this Bible study?"

They consented. I said, "Let me show you how to look up the first verse." I showed them how to use the index, look up the book of the Bible, the chapter, and then the verse—just as if they were beginners, which they were. We looked up John 1:12. "What would the answer be?"

They said, "We'd be a child of God or a son of God."

And I filled it in. I said, "All right, now can you do the rest of those questions, after you've done this one?"

I pointed out the brief directions for living a Christian life on the back of the first Bible study folder and asked them to memorize the verse printed at the end of the study. When they had agreed to all this, I asked them if they could have the study completed by the next evening. They were agreeable. Then I suggested it might be well if each of them did their own study. They could find and discuss their answers together, but they would grow more if each of them wrote his or her own set of answers. They liked that idea too.

Before we had gone on the call that night, we agreed that if Fred and Patty found the Lord, Tom would do the follow-up with them. Now, in the presence of the Tuckers, I asked Tom if he would meet with them tomorrow night to go over their Bible study answers and see if they had any questions. He said that he'd be glad to do so and asked them about an appropriate time for him to stop by.

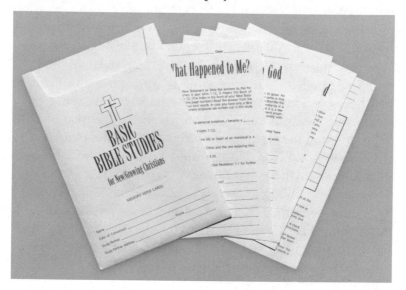

The Bible study I had given to Fred and Patty was the first in the series *Basic Bible Studies for New/Growing Christians* (VE-80),[4] titled "What Happened to Me?" (VE-81). It emphasizes the steps leading to one's conversion. This study is appropriately given to a Christian right after his conversion. The first study should be removed from the rest of the studies in the packet and carried by the personal evangelist.

When folded once, it will fit nicely inside the cover of a coat-pocket-size New Testament. It would fit into a woman's purse.

It is important to *ask* the convert if he or she is willing to do the Bible study. When the answer is affirmative, set a specific day and time when you will get together with the new Christian to go over the study. The convert's agreement for the follow-up worker to meet with him or her at a specific time makes it easy for the worker to return to the home. The follow-up person is merely keeping an agreement to meet the new Christian friend. The setting of an appointment further helps the new convert to have a goal for completing the work. Should the convert fail to have the study done, the agreed-upon appointment becomes the means of administering loving spiritual discipline.

The younger a child is, the more frequently parental attention is needed. Thus the follow-up worker ought to seek the convert's agreement to complete the Bible study within 24 hours and permission to return to go over it. If that is impractical, then the worker should seek completion within 48 hours. Experience has taught us that the more time that elapses between a person's acceptance of Christ as Savior and the beginning of follow-up work, the more difficult it is to do the follow-up. We should start this ministry immediately.

To summarize, the first four steps in follow-up are:

1. Sharing an *assurance verse,* such as John 6:47, with the new convert.

2. Presenting a *Spiritual Birth Certificate* to the convert.

3. Obtaining his or her promise to go to church and make *public testimony* of a newfound relationship with Christ.

4. Obtaining the agreement to begin a *Bible study,* such as *Basic Bible Studies.*

Altar Converts and Others

The procedure that has been described in this chapter to this point is typical for personal evangelism situations.

However, those who find Christ through public evangelism need to be followed up as well. *Basic Bible Studies'* first leaflet, "What Happened to Me?" ought to be distributed at the altar. After one has prayed to receive Christ there, he or she ought to be given that first Bible study; the altar worker should get the name and address; and an appointment should be made for a follow-up worker to call in the convert's home. Extra copies of "What Happened to Me?" (VE-81) may be purchased from Beacon Hill Press of Kansas City so that such a thing may be done without breaking up whole packets.[5]

Basic Bible Studies are also useful for Christians other than brand-new converts. Some Christians may not have developed the habit of regular Bible reading and thus suffer from spiritual anemia. They may be encouraged to do *Basic Bible Studies* and will grow under the program of meeting with a follow-up worker. One pastor reported good response from a Christian who did her first Bible study six months after her conversion. A youth pastor stated that his teens who had been Christians for some time were enthusiastic about the studies. Another pastor reported good results with prospects who had early tasted God's grace, slipped away, and recently renewed their commitment to Christ.

When a conversion occurs in a home, a Personal Evangelism Visit Results Form[6] ought to be filled out and turned in to the one responsible for the local congregation's personal evangelism program. Information on beginning follow-up is included in this form. Further responsibility should be established for the contacting of the follow-up director, so that the convert's name can be recorded on the Follow-up Session Summary,[7] and decisions can be made on future follow-up arrangements by someone with an overall view. The pastor should be contacted so that he or she may be sure that opportunity is given in the morning service for the new convert to make a public profession.

Altar workers need to be aware of the meaning of a convert's coming forward for a public profession. The new convert should not be dealt with as a sinner. Often it is wise for the pastor to announce when such people come to the altar: "This past Thursday evening Fred and Patty opened their hearts to Christ in their home. They are coming forward this morning as public testimony to their acceptance of Christ."

At the altar, the recent convert should be asked some questions that give opportunity for his or her testimony, such as, "Fred [Patty], where is Christ right now?" If the testimony is clear and positive, then a prayer of thanksgiving ought to be offered for what God has done. Should there be confusion or uncertainty in his or her testimony, this time at the altar is an ideal chance to help that one to faith and assurance.

The Fred and Patty Miracle

New people such as Fred and Patty have to be dealt with on a basis they understand. Though intelligent people, they did not know what an "altar call" was; so the meaning of the altar was carefully explained. It was not assumed that they would know what it meant to be "born again." In dealing with the unsaved or newly saved, we must be loving enough to use the language they understand.

"What transpired later in the life of Fred and Patty?" you may wonder. The night after their conversion, the follow-up worker called on them. Each of them had the Bible study completed, and their testimony was vital. Sunday they were in Sunday School and morning worship (only their second time in a Nazarene church). They went to the altar as a public testimony to their conversion. The congregation rejoiced. They grew so much spiritually that they joined the church by profession of faith in May, three months after their acceptance of Christ. Perhaps the best way to make real God's grace in their lives is to include Patty's testimony, written three weeks after becoming a Christian:

Analyzing what opening my heart to Christ has meant to me at first seemed like dissecting a beautiful flower. But I found each petal is individually beautiful and serves to enhance the others.

The first petal of God's love was happiness. February 13, at 11 P.M., I was happier than I've ever been. I believe what amplified the initial happiness was knowing this particular happiness is enduring. Knowing that Jesus has given me a place in heaven gives me daily happiness.

Understanding this, God's second petal of love to me was perspective—for myself and my surroundings. The few material things I have that I thought of as valuable are now reduced to "interesting" and "pretty." When held up to the light of heaven, I realized material things looked pretty dull. I have found that I'm "portable" now. Everything I have of *real* value I carry inside me. As for *self*-perspective, it's clear I am spiritually very young. When I look at my little boy and think how much he has to learn mentally, it occurs to me that God must be looking at me and my spiritual development in much the same way. But just as I love my little boy, I know that God has a love for us, His children, much beyond our comprehension.

I am beginning to realize His love should be likened to my flower's stem, from which all the petals grow. It makes me sad to think that at times I might have bruised that stem by disobeying God. But now that I've opened my heart to Christ, His love gives me strength and enthusiasm to try to understand and follow His Word.

His third petal was of purpose and patience. I want so much to let this light within me shine so brightly that others less fortunate than I could feel the warmth of God's family and join us. It's so comfortable being in God's hands, but it's restless, too, because I want others to accept Christ's gift. But I have accepted a patience within me that He will show me how I may help.

The next petal of this beautiful flower is faith. It constantly amazes me how my faith continues to grow when I thought it was at its peak. Reading the Bible not only reinforces my faith but also adds to it. At first I had only questions, but now the Bible is showing me answers too.

So these are the petals of my spiritual flower so far: happiness, purpose, patience, perspective, love, and faith. In the heavenly alphabet, I believe that spells "New Life." I don't mean to imply these petals are fully developed; I hope to grow a whole spiritual garden.

But this picture is incomplete. After two days of wondering and thinking and self-probing, God saw fit for me to realize the obvious answer. That void is filled by you and your spiritual gardens.

Besides the physical family God has given me, I believe that when I opened my heart to Christ, He blessed me with a spiritual family. A family in which I can draw strength from your joyful commitment, and perhaps you can draw strength from me—if not from what I say, then from the fact I am here trying to express my gratitude for the joy of God and am not where I was a month ago.[8]

For life like this, we're convinced those first four steps of follow-up were worthwhile!

QUESTIONS FOR DISCUSSION

1. What is the purpose of the Spiritual Birth Certificate? Who should sign this certificate?

2. How significant is it to have the new convert make a public confession of his or her recent commitment to Christ?

3. Why is it important for the new convert to begin Bible study right away?

4. How do you use *Basic Bible Studies* with a new or growing Christian?

5. How should altar workers deal with the new Christian who comes to make a public confession of his or her new experience in Christ?

CHAPTER 3

What Do Babies Need?

BOTH PHYSICAL AND SPIRITUAL BABIES HAVE NEED FOR LOVE, nourishment, protection, and training. Let's look first at the need for love. Waylon Moore, highly regarded for his book *New Testament Follow-up for Pastors and Laymen,* has said, "Spiritual parents are to love their children as Christ loved them; this love is the basic necessity for successful parenthood, and is usually missing in follow-up that fails."[1]

Jesus said, "My command is this: Love each other as I have loved you" (John 15:12). John wrote, "This is how we know what love is: Jesus Christ laid down his life for us. And we ought to lay down our lives for our brothers" (1 John 3:16). Perhaps only a few of us will be called to lay down our lives to the death in following up a convert, but we will be called upon to lay down a part of our lives. We will lay down a chunk of time, we will put out effort and energy that would otherwise be saved, we will open ourselves up to bleed due to heartbreak and disappointment.

The prayer I pray most often for follow-up workers is: *O God, give them a parent heart.* Paul spoke of the scarcity of parent hearts when he stated, "Even though you have ten thousand guardians in Christ, you do not have many fathers, for in Christ Jesus I became your father through the gospel" (1 Cor. 4:15).

Babies who are not nourished soon die. The babe in Christ needs the right food (the Word of God) and in a form that he or she is able to digest (anything from "milk" to "meat" is available). The capacities and rate of intake of babies are limited; so we feed with a bottle, not with a fire hose. At first, the spiritual baby is fed through the constant attention of a parent. But as he or she grows, the child may be taught right eating habits and the choice of proper food. In maturity, he or she will in turn be able to feed others.

Protection is needed. Imagine if your five-year-old daughter did not arrive home from kindergarten at the usual 3:15 in the afternoon. About 7:00 that evening you would not simply muse to yourself, "If Miriam doesn't get home by 11:00 tonight, I'm going out to look for her." Of course not; you can't even imagine such a thing. Yet how is it we will be unconcerned about our spiritual children when they miss meeting us at church as they promised?

"Your enemy the devil prowls around like a roaring lion looking for someone to devour" (1 Pet. 5:8). The newborn child of God is a tender prey for the devil. The new Christian must be taught how to "resist the devil" so that he will flee (James 4:7). The spiritual parent's example of faith will give the spiritual infant a shield to quench flaming arrows (Eph. 6:16). A major duty of that parent is to teach the child how to meet temptation with the Word (v. 17).

Babies need training. Their ultimate goal is adulthood, not continual infancy. Moore says, "Walking in victory and witnessing for Christ comprise the New Testament objectives of the training of the new believers."[2]

Four Channels of Supply

The New Testament describes four ways the early Christian leaders supplied the needs of love, nourishment, protection, and training of their converts. The first of these is personal contact. Jesus exemplified this in the time He spent with the Twelve. From His group of disciples, He chose the Twelve to be apostles (Luke 6:13). According to Mark 3:14, the purpose of appointing these Twelve was "that they might be with him and that he might send them out to preach." The personal contact, or "with him" principle, is emphasized in Jesus' words to His disciples: "You also must testify, for you have been with me from the beginning" (John 15:27).

Frequently a list of people is given in Acts of individuals who accompanied Paul on his journeys. The apostle used these times together to disciple men. When he had seven men "with him" in 20:4 (many trans.), he was strengthening Christians and preparing spiritual leaders for four different cities. Paul expressed to Barnabas his follow-up concern for new converts when he said, "Let us go back and visit the brothers in all the towns where we preached the word of the Lord and see how they are doing" (15:36). Just as Christ and Paul found time to spend with their disciples, so must we with our new Christians.

Personal prayer is a second channel by which establishing grace flows to new Christians. The night before His crucifixion, Christ interceded for the protection of His disciples in His absence (John 17:15). Paul began many of his letters with a reference to his constant intercession for new believers (see Phil. 1:3-6 and 1 Thess. 1:2-3). Waylon Moore says , "If a man is interceding, he *will* follow up."[3]

To the Philippians, Paul wrote, "I hope in the Lord Jesus to send Timothy to you soon, that I also may be cheered when I receive news about you. I have no one else like him, who takes a genuine interest in your welfare" (2:19-20). Imprisoned in Rome, Paul was unable to visit his spiritual children. So he sent Timothy as his personal representative. Since Timothy was "likeminded" (KJV) in his concern for the Christians, he was an adequate representative. This third method, the personal representative, is the basis of the present practice of using an adoptive spiritual parent in follow-up.

The fourth channel to supply new convert needs is personal correspondence. Much of the New Testament consists of letters to encourage and establish new believers in their faith. Paul dealt with all sorts of problems that would sidetrack believers. In a touching passage in 1 Thess. 3:1-8, he rejoices at the news that his converts remain in the faith:

> Therefore when we could bear it no longer, we were willing to be left behind at Athens alone, and we sent Timo-

thy, our brother and God's servant in the gospel of Christ, to establish you in your faith and to exhort you, that no one be moved by these afflictions. You yourselves know that this is to be our lot. For when we were with you, we told you beforehand that we were to suffer affliction; just as it has come to pass, and as you know. For this reason, when I could bear it no longer, I sent that I might know your faith, for fear that somehow the tempter had tempted you and that our labor would be in vain.

But now that Timothy has come to us from you, and has brought us the good news of your faith and love and reported that you always remember us kindly and long to see us, as we long to see you—for this reason, brethren, in all our distress and affliction we have been comforted about you through your faith; for now we live, if you stand fast in the Lord (RSV).

Peter (2 Pet. 1:12-15) and Luke (Luke 1:3-4) wrote with follow-up concerns at heart. Today a letter by a Christian to a new convert too far away to visit personally can be a means of spiritual establishment. Bible studies can be sent in the mail, and personal letters can be bathed in the Scriptures and over-flowing with encouragement. The telephone, tape recorder, and E-mail are other non-face-to-face methods that can be highly profitable.

Everyone Needs Parents

When children are born into the physical world, it is God's plan for them to have parents. In the spiritual realm the plan is the same. Through the close communion of the Bride (the Church, Body of Believers) with the Bridegroom (Jesus Christ), spiritual children have been born. Christ watches over these children through the work of the Holy Spirit as one phase of their protection. But He expects the Church, as the Bride, to assume her share of parental responsibility. So an individual member or members of the Church must show loving concern for that new Christian.

If, in the physical realm, the parents of a child are suddenly killed, government agencies move in to be sure the child is provided adoptive parents to take their place. In the spiritual realm, the person most responsible for a spiritual baby's birth may not be able, due to other heavy Kingdom responsibilities or because of his or her high reproduction rate, to care for the new convert. He or she may be so used of God in bringing new souls to Christ that it would not be possible to keep up with all the spiritual children produced.

So there is a need for spiritual adoptive parents—ones not primarily responsible for the spiritual infant's birth, but with a parent heart and a willingness to take on the heavy responsibility of nurturing the newborn. If children, whether physical or spiritual, are neglected by parents, there are two possible results—they become delinquent or die.

In the life of any baby, the first days are most crucial. Thus *Basic Bible Studies* are geared to be used during a spiritual child's first seven or eight weeks. The first study, "What Happened to Me?" is to be given to the convert at the time of his conversion, with the follow-up worker to check back within 24 hours (or at the most 48 hours). At the time the spiritual parent goes back to go over the first Bible study, the second study is given the convert, and an appointment is made to check that study a week later. Usually studies two through eight are given and checked at one-week intervals.

Babies and Bible Studies

There are some needs of the spiritually young that have shaped the writing and use of *Basic Bible Studies*. Realizing that in the first 10 days of a child's physical life a mother is almost constantly with her baby, we gear ourselves for our most intense spiritual attention in the first days of spiritual life.

Perhaps I can describe this urgency from a current example. Thursday night I called on Joe and Sally Martin, who have been attending our church recently. With me were Harry and Lori, the Martins' next-door neighbors who first brought them to church; and Len, who is one of our youth workers and especially interested in helping the teenage daughter of the home. At 10 P.M. Thursday, with tears and rejoicing, Joe and Sally accepted Christ. It is now noon on Saturday. So far these 38 hours have been filled with these activities of follow-up attention:

1. All members of the calling team have been praying for Joe and Sally.

2. Lori returned Friday night, found each had completed their first Bible study, heard Sally quote Rev. 3:20 from memory and Joe nearly quote his (he had taken his New Testament to work with him but had a hectic day at the office— so he was a little short on the memory verse).

3. On Saturday, Lori was spending time with Sally, talking of God's ways.

4. I telephoned and talked to Sally to see how they were coming along spiritually. Sally told me they'd found peace, and Christ was giving them a new life.

5. Lori has arranged for Dean and Mary to come by and check over the next two Bible studies with Joe and Sally, since Harry and Lori will be on vacation.

6. I phoned the follow-up director, reported this conversion, told him who would do the follow-up, and recorded the names of Joe and Sally on the Follow-up Session Summary.[4]

Within the next 30 hours I expect to see the following:

1. Joe and Sally will be in Sunday School, and their class will discover their new faith and surround them with love.

2. In the morning service, they will go forward for public testimony. I have already contacted the preacher of the morning, so an appropriate opportunity for an invitation can be given. When Joe and Sally give this testimony, immediately others will begin surrounding them with prayer and concern.

3. When Joe and Sally return to the evening service, people will be greeting them with words of encouragement.

This may all seem rather detailed, but it is offered to demonstrate parental concern in the spiritual realm and the special attention needed by spiritual children in their earliest days. And what did Sally say in our phone conversation of a few minutes ago? "I can't get over all this loving attention that's been shown to us."

And there are other baby needs to which the *Basic Bible Studies* speak. Most follow-up Bible studies are part of a booklet of studies with a total of 20 or more pages. *Basic Bible Studies* are in separate leaflets on purpose—so that the spiritual baby may be given one at a time and not be overwhelmed with too much at once.

When James became a Christian, someone told him to read the Bible. He began in Genesis and got hung up on all the "begats." *Basic Bible Studies* deals with the most needed areas for successful Christian living. A new Christian should not have to wait months to find out how to resist temptation—so that is covered in the second study. A young Christian would be in trouble if he or she had to wait six months to hear the pastor preach on how to pray. The new convert can be learning that on the fourth study.

In addition to the *Basic Bible Studies* for adults, *Now That I'm a Christian: Basic Bible Studies for Youth* (YD-501)[5] will meet the needs of teens. For those younger, there is *Now That I'm a Christian: Basic Bible Studies for Children* (VE-50).[6] It is well for

us to remember that we should adjust to our convert's pace. Some will want to do two studies a week, while some, more limited, will do well at one every two weeks. Though normally the once-a-week practice will be best, we must remember that our primary task is helping *people,* not filling in Bible study blanks.

The questions of the studies are asked in such a way as to require the personal involvement of the convert in the answer. Bible study will only have deep value for a convert when he or she is able to make personal application of the truth learned; mere factual knowledge is not enough. Thus many questions will include the words "I" and "we." For example, one question is "What should we do when the devil attacks us? (James 4:7)."

Person-to-Person

Dr. James Kennedy has said that in establishing converts, fellowship is as important as the Word.[7] In the physical life, we certainly know that it is not only the milk the baby is fed but also the security created by being held by the mother that is important to an infant's full development.

Let us think about fellowship as it relates to the establishing of converts. In all of Christian work, and especially in follow-up, we need to develop such a person-to-person approach that individuals will feel valued for their own sakes, and not viewed as potential customers for the church.

The local church will need to make specific effort to gear itself for the conservation of new converts. This will include developing among the present constituency an understanding of the new convert's point of view. The new convert does not understand all the language of Zion yet, nor will he or she immediately live up to all the holiness ethic of a mature saint. Established Christians must be loving and patient about these matters. A Sunday School class for new Christians may be a good idea instead of dropping that three-day-old Christian into a class studying Ezekiel. It's rough on a new convert to get caught in the middle of Ezekiel's wheels.

Besides changing the local church's mind-set, we must develop ways for the local church to show love. Many times Christians have love they would like to share, but the channels for expression of love are not there. Leadership has the responsibility for developing those channels. To open our minds to possibilities here, let me give a brief listing of the 14 committees or organizations used at one local church and the purpose of each. In this listing, note the recurring emphasis on new people and the demonstration of love possibilities.

Outreach Emphasis	*Purpose*
1. Hospitality	To help visitors feel at home in our services
2. Special Interest Groups	To reach out through groups, built around a special interest, to new people
3. Personal Evangelism	To share the gospel on a person-to-person basis
4. Follow-up	To direct new converts in Bible study in order to establish them in their faith
5. Home Bible Study	To promote Bible studies in homes, both to encourage Christian growth and reach the unconverted
6. Correspondence	To communicate by letter with those in special need as revealed through the news media
7. Youth	To promote the reaching of teens with the gospel
8. Friendship Registration	To gather and distribute the important information from the weekly Friendship Registration pad[8]

9. Prayer	To send periodically prayer requests to the small groups
10. Pie Ministry	To make friendship calls and deliver baked goods to local people who visit our church
11. Sunday School Outreach	To develop new classes to reach out to new people
12. Special Events	To organize occasional special events to promote our outreach ministries
13. Small Groups	To lead the various small groups to communicate care and prayer and both disciple and evangelize
14. Altar Work	To guide the work done with seekers around the altar so that they receive the greatest spiritual help[9]

And then, especially, the local church will need to develop a follow-up program with trained adoptive spiritual parents who will give each convert a loving heart and direction in the Word. Waylon Moore proclaims, "All follow-up is directed in the New Testament toward the needs of the individual."[10]

This individual attention is heightened by the format of *Basic Bible Studies.* The adoptive spiritual parent will be calling once a week over a seven-week period after the first study has been given. The fact that the follow-up worker has the next Bible study to give the convert is his or her natural entree into the home.

Neal was a plumber in his late 20s when he and his wife found Christ in their home. Another couple, about their age, and Christians just over a year, were assigned to Neal and Wendy for follow-up. Neal said he learned the importance of

Christian friends and that it was an ideal situation to meet with this young couple with whom they had so much in common. They would even plan their once-a-week meetings alternating between their homes and having their after-supper dessert together.

The adoptive spiritual parent should take the responsibility of sitting with the new Christian in worship services and of introducing him or her to other Christians. Fred and Patty emphasized these values in their new Christian life in a letter they wrote. They said, "A wonderful plus to the Bible studies was fellowship with other Christians. We looked forward to our weekly get-together to review our completed study. . . . On one occasion our Bible study 'guide' brought two Christian friends with him for us to meet, and the evening was filled with sharing and caring and mutual testimony of how the Lord had blessed our lives."

And the Word!

Don't forget the value of getting that convert regularly into the Word of God. You will notice that all references to the Old Testament in *Basic Bible Studies* are quoted. This is so you may provide New Testaments for those who do not have Bibles in their home. If many Bibles were supplied by a local church, the cost would become prohibitive. Most, however, can afford inexpensive paperback New Testaments. Thus with your church's gift of a New Testament and *Basic Bible Studies* with Old Testament passages quoted, the convert can do all the questions.

When one is a new Christian, he or she is usually very teachable. The convert must have direction in the Word of God that will not lead him or her astray. One new Christian said she was so hungry for spiritual truth that she would have looked to anyone who talked of God. While we are trying to lead the new Christian over certain biblical truth on a topic-by-topic basis, he or she is also being asked to read portions of

John's Gospel. The hope here is that a pattern of systematically reading through entire books of the Bible will be developed.

One of the goals of *Basic Bible Studies* is to build a habit of life that includes daily Bible study. Wendy, as a new Christian having done *Basic Bible Studies,* said the program made her start reading the Bible regularly. Probably this is a result of having a specific Bible study to do and the discipline of having it done by a specific time to meet her appointment with her follow-up worker.

Patty's analysis of what the Bible study meant to Fred and her was:

> With the saving experience we felt a need to search out God's will through the Scriptures, but didn't know where to start. The studies gave us that direction, which led to independent reading. . . . The studies did not assume we were acquainted with . . . correct procedure for completing a Bible study. . . . We appreciated the simplicity of the studies. We felt they kept our interest but weren't so deep as to discourage us. . . . Several times we remarked how uncanny the correlation was between the Word emphasized in the Bible studies and our Christian growth. . . . I . . . remember this happening with regard to Bible Study No. 8. We were asked to give our testimonies. I prepared mine, but it seemed incomplete. For days this bothered me, and finally I realized the missing element in my testimony of thanksgiving was the loving Christians who were entering our lives. The Bible study we received some days later was No. 8, which stressed the importance of our spiritual family in the church. This "uncanny correlation" was in fact proof that we have one unchanging God who speaks to all of us about the Truth. It was this type of reinforcement that made us feel we were truly following the Way.

QUESTIONS FOR DISCUSSION

1. What are the four basic needs of both physical and spiritual infants?

2. How did the leaders of the Early Church meet the needs of new converts?

3. How significant in the life of the new convert can the ministry of adoptive spiritual parents be?

4. What is your reaction to the statement that Christian fellowship is as important as Bible study in the establishment of a new believer?

5. Why must established Christians be loving and patient with new converts?

6. What type of channels can leadership provide to help Christians share their love and concern for others?

CHAPTER 4

The Adventure of a Follow-up Call

YOU HAVE AN APPOINTMENT TO GO BACK to your new convert to go over his first Bible study. You wonder—what happens on a follow-up call? Many of your questions will be answered by a set of "General Instructions," which include information that will apply to any follow-up call you might make (see appendix).[1] These ought to be reviewed before each call. Then there are the "Special Instructions," which give more specialized direction as they apply to unique aspects of each study. Reviewing the instructions for the specific study you will be checking on a given call will give you added confidence. But some basic guidelines about a follow-up call should be considered here.

Help the Convert Talk

You will want to conduct the follow-up session with your convert's point of view uppermost in your mind. You will want to protect him or her from needless embarrassment. If a husband and wife have both accepted Christ together, there is no problem in dealing with both of them at the same time. If you are following up a teenager, who may be the only Christian in the family, it may be difficult for him or her to discuss the Bible study in the parents' presence. It may be best to pick the teen up, go out for Cokes, and discuss the study.

Spend part of your time together to renew your acquaintance. Then a rather general and open-ended question about a man's spiritual life, such as "How have things gone for you spiritually today, Bill?" will help him to be free to share his feelings. Often this is a time of victorious testimony. Sometimes this leads to a sharing of problems you need to hear. To introduce the review of the convert's Bible study, you could say, with an expectant enthusiasm, "Bill, did the Bible study help you?" Regardless of what his response might be, you could say, "Well, let's look at it together."

You will skim through his answers quickly, pausing to talk about every third or fourth answer, if they seem correct. If he has missed the main meaning of a question, you might say something like this: "Bill, that's an interesting answer you have here, but there's another main thought behind this verse. Let's look it up together." Use the translation he used. Talk about it together. Ask him to quote his memory verse to you. Your total length of time needed for a call is 20 to 40 minutes. Often these follow-up sessions are times of such spiritual blessing and warm friendship that they may be longer.

More than Filling in the Blank

When you go to your new convert to review the results of the first study, you leave the second study. It is during this session that you leave the colored packet and explain to your convert how he or she may use this packet in which to store all the completed studies. Be sure, as his or her spiritual parent, you write your name, address, and phone number on the packet and urge the convert to call you any time he or she has need.

Basic Bible Studies were prepared so you can find the right answer with at least nine different Bible translations. It was discovered early in their preparation that there would be serious problems if the studies were written on the basis of only one translation. With so many translations in existence today, it would be common for the new convert to use a translation different enough in wording from the one upon which the questions were based that he or she couldn't figure out the correct answer.

The nine translations usable for these studies are: King James Version, *Revised Standard Version, New American*

Standard Bible, Today's English Version, The Living Bible, New English Bible, New International Version, Douay Version (which is the old Catholic version), and the *New American Bible* (which is a new Catholic version).

The latter two are not attempts to get people to study the Catholic Bible; they are given so that the follow-up person need not argue with the convert who has had a Roman Catholic background and is tied to his or her Bible and not able to immediately accept the Protestant Bible. Give a Bible study that the new Christian can do with a Catholic Bible and still find answers that will help in his or her Christian life.

As you go over your convert's answers on a given study, write an encouraging phrase beside those where he or she has shown an especially good insight. "Praise God" is an appropriate exclamation to write on the study margin. Let your verbal comments on various answers be an opportunity for him or her to ask further questions.

After you have gone through the entire study together, write across the top "excellent" or "very good" or "good." Never mark a study lower than "good." If half of this new believer's answers are wrong, it's real "good" to know that for the first time in life, he or she is studying the Bible. Your goal is his or her spiritual encouragement, not just academic rating.

On any given answer written by the convert, the follow-up worker's concern should not simply be whether the blank on the piece of paper is filled with an acceptable answer. Endeavor to discover what he or she really means. If to the question, "Where is Jesus right now?" the new Christian writes, "I think He's in my heart," I'd talk about that answer. It seems to suggest doubt or a lack of assurance. Help the convert discover the full privilege of assurance. Your goal is not doing the lesson primarily; it is helping a person. The lesson is simply a tool for accomplishing that end.

Frequently the increased sensitivity of a new convert's conscience will cause that one to begin asking questions about ethical issues in his or her own life. Questions I've been asked include, "Is social drinking wrong for a Christian?" or, "Do you think it's right for me to go to the movies?" Rather than giving a straight yes or no, it is better to help the individual discover a spiritual principle and then ask the new convert to tell you what he or she thinks should be done as a Christian. The principle given in lesson one, "What would Jesus do?" is a good one to refer to again and again.

The advantage in dealing with personal convictions this way is that you are: (1) helping your convert to learn to live by unchanging principles; (2) letting him or her make decisions, which is a maturing experience; (3) allowing growth at his or her rate of speed (too much too soon will scare the convert off—we don't expect first graders on their first day of arithmetic to be able to do long division); and (4) allowing the greatest possibilities for the Holy Spirit's leadership.

Years ago I was going over *Basic Bible Studies* with my daughter Rachel, who at the time was a seventh grader. She had found a good relationship with the Lord in girls' camp the previous summer and was doing these Bible studies as follow-up. We were on the fifth study, which is on stewardship, where the key verse is "So whether you eat or drink or whatever you do, do it all for the glory of God" (1 Cor. 10:31).

I told Rachel that when I became a Christian, I could no longer put a cigarette in my mouth and say, "O dear God, bless this cigarette to my body's strength and to Your glory," and pray grace over the cigarette as I pray grace over my food. I said, "So I quit smoking." I added, "You know, you can use that test on everything. So of the places we go we say, 'Do I glorify God by going here?' Of the clothes I wear I ask, 'Do I glorify God by the clothes I wear?' The things I say, the things I listen to, the things I watch"—we just went through every area of life and asked ourselves this question, "Does it glorify God?"

Rachel got so excited to get this one great concept that she could apply to all her actions. Does it glorify God?

Does it glorify God? Does it glorify God? She learned a concept, but she didn't learn it until we talked about it. It's not just the matter of the actual questions in the eight studies, but it's the matter of your sharing with the convert. You see, the convert not only needs the Word but also needs you.

Disappointment and Discipline

Specific assignments are highly important in order to give the convert a goal to aim at. And discipline is important if he (John) fails to carry out his intentions. If you have the convert's agreement for you to come by on Friday night at seven o'clock to review the Bible study, but it has not been done, you've got to discipline the convert. You don't, of course, put him over your knee and spank him.

After discovering the convert was neglectful, you might say, "John, I'm disappointed in you not having your Bible study done. You know, John, reading the Word of God is so important that I can't help being concerned when you skip it. I believe, though, you will be serious about this, and you really do want to grow in your Christian life." Somehow your firmness and love have to be mixed together. Then you set another appointment, by which time he promises to have the study done. You look up three or four answers together to be sure he understands how to do this study and to give him a bit of spiritual truth.

Of course, there is a point of spiritual neglect or rebellion by a new convert in which it is difficult to help him or her spiritually. Imagine Tom as a new professing Christian. He must be willing to grow, to study, to obey God. He differs from a physical baby in this regard. Some things you can do for a physical baby to help him or her whether the baby wants you to or not, but it is not so with spiritual babies. This is why it is important to minister by permission. You ask Tom upon his conversion if he is willing to do the Bible study; you set an appointment time acceptable to him; on each call you confirm your appointment for a call back. If the convert is giving me signals he is no longer willing to do the Bible study, I try to help him see the results of his decision and allow him the privilege of deciding to no longer continue in the study program.

It is a bit sad to talk about this, but we must be realistic. Jesus was the best follow-up Worker, but He had Judas. Paul had Demas. Jesus taught in the parable of the soils that some would receive the Word of God readily and later wither away or be choked out (Matt. 13:1-23). Let us be sure that any falling away is the convert's decision and not our neglect.

When a spiritual baby seems to be experiencing difficulty, it is best to send the spiritual parent back on the next follow-up call along with the adoptive spiritual parent. Usually the one most responsible for the new Christian's spiritual birth will have the greatest influence on the convert. There may be times when the follow-up director may need to assign a new spiritual adoptive parent to the case if the problem is due to a lack of concern or ability by the present worker. With the admission that some spiritual babies die, we do well to rejoice in the fact that the majority of these spiritual children, when loved and cared for, will thrive and grow.

Weapons That Produce Life

The two major weapons of the spiritual adoptive parent are the Word of God and personal testimony. When the convert asks you a question, answer from the Bible, not just to give a specific answer on that question from the Bible, but to begin to develop the concept that the young Christian can find the answers for problems in the Word of God. As that spiritual child learns the Word, he or she will find ability to resist the devil by the Word as Jesus did in the wilderness (Matt. 4:1-11).

Urge the spiritual baby to do scripture memorization. There is a memory verse in each Bible study. The baby Christian cuts it out, carries it in a wallet or pocket, and does memory work. Hiding the Word of God in the heart protects from sin (Ps. 119:11). After these verses are memorized, there is a little slot in the colored packet where they can be stored.

The parent's personal testimony is important, for that communicates to the spiritual child that the God who inspired the Bible in centuries past is working in a life today. The Bible says you can resist temptation; you tell how God helped you resist. The Bible says God answers prayer; you testify to the answer to prayer you had yesterday. The Bible says God makes all things work together for good for those who love Him; you reveal how difficult situations in your life were used by God for your growth. Rev. 12:11 says, "They overcame him [the devil] by the blood of the Lamb and by the word of their testimony."

Discussing the Word and sharing testimony is made possible by the week-by-week personal contact. After Wendy had done all eight lessons, she looked back and rejoiced that with these studies she'd had regular contact for two months with another Christian. Sometimes the spiritual parent with a busy schedule is tempted to set appointments with the new convert after Wednesday service or after a Sunday service. It is better than not having any time to meet to discuss Bible study—but the opportunity to meet with the convert at another time is no doubt more valuable. It gives him or her Sunday and Wednesday exposure to the Word and Christian friends, and then on another day, like Friday, the new Christian has a third exposure when you come by to do Bible study. Usually the after-Sunday session is not as relaxed because time pressures are upon you.

Once in a while a new Christian will have such a good grasp of the lesson that the spiritual adoptive parent will be tempted to give all the remaining lessons in a group so that the convert can do several a week. As soon as the adoptive parent has made this move, however, he or she has eliminated a good reason for weekly fellowship with the convert and reduced the convert's opportunities for week-by-week discipline by having a deadline to meet.

Ken did very well on his first lesson. The follow-up worker felt he had a good grasp of the Scriptures, so the worker gave him the bulk of the studies. We were never able to determine after that how Ken was progressing. There was no check back, no reporting, a limiting of the Christian fellowship he needed. Now he is not attending our church, though he gave a clear testimony at the time of his conversion.

How It Was with Chad

Many of the truths about good follow-up methods are wrapped up in one of the first structured follow-up sessions in which I became involved. Let me tell you about it.

I began calling on a converted dope addict in the county jail. His name was Chad Smith. He wasn't converted through any effort of mine, but a Baptist lady called me and told me he had been converted, and he needed someone to follow up. So I went to call on him. He accepted me right away; he was so hungry for a Christian brother. God had delivered him instantaneously from his heroin addiction, which had controlled him for two years. He was in jail because he had turned himself in to the police for a burglary he had committed to get money to support his dope habit.

I gave him the first Bible study and said, "Now I'll be back to visit you each week, Chad. Do you think you can have this done near the end of the week?" He said, "Sure." I came back, yet it wasn't done. But I'd left it general, "near the end of the week." I said, "OK, Chad, I'm coming back next week, and I'll plan to visit you every Friday afternoon after I have finished with my classes. In order to be sure this is done, you have it done Friday morning; always have it done Friday morning." And I gave him a specific time.

The next week he had his study done. As a matter of fact, in those few weeks since he had been converted, he had been studying the Bible so much he answered every question from memory on the first sheet without even opening his Bible. And then he did the second one.

Chad told me that when God saved him, He delivered him from the dope habit. But as we were going over the second study, he said, "You know, Chic, I want to be so strong that if one of my best buddies should come up and offer me free dope, free heroin, I'd turn it down." He didn't tell me he was having a battle. He'd said earlier he had been delivered; now he was saying that if someone should come and offer him dope, well, he wasn't too sure as to the outcome.

When you deal with a person like this, you have to read between the lines, as with any convert. They don't just come out and say, "I'm starting to have a spiritual battle." You have got to listen to what they're saying in words and what they're saying by their feelings. I figured—Chad is telling me that he's having a battle. So I said, "Chad, you know when I first became a Christian, I had certain sins in my life that had such control on me, I didn't see how I could overcome them. But do you know that God gave me such victory that not once in 17 years have I ever gone back to those sins. And if He did that for me, He can do it for you."

We talked about the meaning of 1 Cor. 10:13. "God says, 'No temptation has seized you except what is common to man. And God is faithful; *he will not let you be tempted beyond what you can bear.* But when you are tempted, he will also provide a way out so that you can stand up under it' [italics mine]. That means that if God allows a temptation to come, He already knows in advance that He's going to give you enough grace to overcome it, or He won't let it come." Chad lit up like a Christmas tree. He said, "That's right." You could just see him gain confidence.

He went through that jail experience. He was there for about 10 weeks, and I called on him each week. By the time he had served his time and was placed on parole, he had witnessed to others in the jail. Three inmates had made professions of faith, and the atmosphere of the whole jail had changed. When they first put him in the trusty tank, a person came up and said, "Hey, you're that Jesus person. We know about people like you here. This whole jail is different since you've come."

Chad was released and got a job. The last time I talked to him, he was earning money to go to Bible college the following January to study to be a preacher. I'm convinced Chad did not fall away because he was followed up. And those sessions together added up to a rewarding spiritual adventure for me. It will be so for you too.

QUESTIONS FOR DISCUSSION

1. What instructions are available for follow-up workers?

2. What nine Bible translations were used in the preparation of *Basic Bible Studies*?

3. What place is there for discipline in this Bible study program?

4. How would you deal with the new convert who becomes rebellious?

5. Why should the new convert memorize the suggested key Bible verses?

6. What are the two major weapons the spiritual adoptive parents can use to help the new convert?

CHAPTER 5

Equipping Saints for Follow-up

IT HAS BEEN SAID THAT THE GREATEST PROBLEM in the Church is the unemployment problem. Some 15 to 20 percent of the members do all the work while other potential leadership rots in the pew.[1] The follow-up of new converts has become an area where many laymen are discovering their gifts and establishing their ministry. Because follow-up is less threatening than personal evangelism, more are willing to try. Because, in one sense, it is not so demanding, more can be used. Because it is a ministry to people, it is both more fulfilling and exciting than painting the chairs in the junior department—although this may need to be done. One follow-up director in a local church testified to the spiritual development of follow-up workers. While helping others, they experienced the leadership of the Spirit and answers to prayer.

The Adoptive Spiritual Parent

A parent heart is the most needed characteristic for those who will follow up spiritual babies. The spiritual parents should possess the spirit of Paul, who wrote, "With such yearning love we chose to impart to you not only the gospel of God but our very selves, so dear had you become to us" (1 Thess. 2:8, NEB). Even the parent's use of follow-up materials should not dilute concern for the spiritual infant. Waylon Moore says, "Rely on literature and you will fail in follow-up; rely on Spirit-taught men and women with a heart for discipling others and literature becomes a useful tool."[2]

Besides love, anyone who is to be an adoptive spiritual parent should have a reasonably pleasing personality and common sense in dealing with people. The characteristic of faithfulness that helps one to stick to a task is needed. Certainly he or she must be a dedicated Christian. Probably it is wiser to choose individuals for this ministry rather than use just anyone who is willing to do it—even as Sunday School teachers must be appointed and cannot just volunteer and begin teaching.

The adoptive parent must be trained too. The hope behind this book is that training in local churches will put tools and love together—and a host of follow-up leaders will be raised up to nurture new Christians. *Basic Bible Studies* are geared for use by trained adoptive spiritual parents. These studies are also to be especially complementary to some of the most fruitful personal evangelism approaches being used today, without being contradictory to any evangelism approach.

Records Can Help

When the convert has received his or her first Bible study, the rest of the studies remain in the white packet in the possession of the spiritual parent. This packet, sitting on the follow-up worker's desk or dresser, is a constant reminder to pray for the spiritual infant and for help with the next appointment. The Record of Progress chart on the envelope,[3] filled in by the parent, indicates the convert's growth.

Each week the follow-up worker should fill out the Convert Follow-up Report Card[4] and deposit it at the designated collection point. This card conveys a great deal of information about the convert's spiritual progress. The follow-up director picks up these cards and records weekly the results on the Follow-up Session Summary.[5]

When a Convert Follow-up Report Card indicates a problem in a spiritual child's life requiring emergency attention, the director calls the pastor. Otherwise, once a month, an up-to-date copy of the Follow-up Session Summary goes to the pastor so that he or she will have a quick picture of the progress of every convert to whom the local church is ministering. If it seems that such records are an unnecessary detail, imagine how one would otherwise keep track of any amount of converts that exceeds 30 in a given year. Usually some are just forgotten.

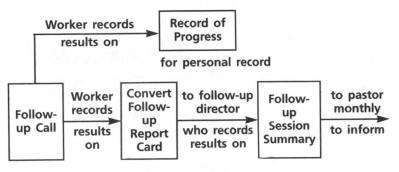

The Follow-up Director

If a pastor begins to have prayers answered and many new souls are born into the kingdom of God, there will be desperate need for trained follow-up workers to help nurture the converts. Also needed will be a follow-up director to coordinate the efforts of the follow-up workers. Every adoption agency needs a director.

Perhaps it is the best summary of the follow-up director's job to say he or she follows up on the follow-up workers. A detailed listing of the director's responsibilities would be helpful and is here included:

Responsibilities of Follow-up Director

1. Pick up Convert Follow-up Report Cards weekly (at follow-up mailbox).

2. Tabulate them on Follow-up Session Summary at home.

3. On the first of each month give an up-to-date copy of the Follow-up Session Summary to the minister of outreach or the pastor.

4. Be sure each new convert is assigned a follow-up worker.

5. Assign a new follow-up worker if another worker is unable to finish an assignment or is ineffective.

6. When a follow-up worker fails to report, check by phone to determine the status of the convert.

7. When a follow-up worker or new convert reports that all eight studies are completed, contact the minister of outreach or the pastor for the awarding of the diploma.[6]

8. Pray regularly for the new converts and follow-up workers.

9. By the time a convert has completed all eight studies, send his name to the small-group director for assignment to a small group.

10. Should especially difficult problems arise that the director is unable to solve, contact the minister of outreach or the pastor.

11. Initiate new follow-up training as needed.

Deciding Who the Parents Will Be

How many children do you feel yourself able to care for in your family? If 15 or 20 seem like too many, do you see why in the spiritual realm one who has been blessed with winning 20 to Christ will need the help of those who will "adopt" some of his or her spiritual children? Normally no follow-up worker should be expected to have more than one assignment with a new Christian (or a new Christian couple) at a time. A husband and wife both trained in follow-up should work as a team. They are especially effective working with a newly converted couple. Seldom should a worker be assigned to relatives who have been saved.

When a personal evangelism call is to be made, the members of the team (most churches with a planned personal evangelism program call in groups of three) should decide among themselves who will do the follow-up if there is a conversion. Then, after the prospects have made a profession of faith, the call leader would ask the one earlier agreed on to come back and do follow-up and seek the agreement of the new converts to this plan of Bible study. The actual dynamics of this situation was spelled out in dealing with converts Fred and Patty as narrated earlier in chapter 2.

Because the Christian worker is present at the spiritual birth, he or she will likely be accepted by the new converts on a return call. This worker goes over Bible study No. 1 and gives the second study to the new converts. When returning to check the second study, he or she brings another Christian. This second Christian is introduced and takes in the events of the study. At the end of the session, the original worker asks permission for the second Christian to come back the next week to check the third study. Thus there has been transfer made from the spiritual parent (or at least one present at the spiritual birth) to the adoptive spiritual parent.

The adoptive spiritual parent is chosen as the result of a conference between the follow-up worker who checked the first study and the follow-up director. It is the responsibility of the follow-up director, on the basis of the current staff of workers, to make the assignment. Often, the pastor and follow-up director will discuss a particular assignment too.

The appointment of a particular follow-up worker will take certain issues into account. For example, matching the new or growing Christian with the most suitable follow-up worker is essential to effective ministry. Such things as age, sex, children, occupations, interests, religious backgrounds should be taken into consideration. The better the match between the convert and the worker, the more effective likely will be the relationship to be established.

The follow-up worker, already trained, is contacted by the follow-up director and asked to take on the responsibility of a spiritual child. The new follow-up worker is given the name of the one doing follow-up to this point, and details are worked out between them for the next time of getting together with the convert.

Back to School Again?

The adoptive spiritual parent needs some classes on how to be a good parent. If you are reading this book, you are probably in training for the job. If personal evangelists take training in spiritual obstetrics, it would be wise for follow-up workers to take training in spiritual pediatrics.

Good follow-up work comes in part from training. Because follow-up is not as threatening as personal evangelism, it is possible to develop workers without on-the-job training. However, more effective follow-up workers can be developed if they can go out with an experienced worker and observe follow-up procedures (this is on-the-job training). The following Follow-up Training Schedule gives direction for a solid experience in learning.

HOMEWORK

WEEK NO.	CLASS SESSION	READING	WRITTEN	MEMORY	ON-THE-JOB TRAINING
1.	"What's Happening at the Back Door?" Discuss *Basic Bible Studies* No. 1.	Through Chapter 1, *Conserve the Converts*	*Basic Bible Studies* Nos. 1 and 2	Rev. 3:20	Observe a follow-up visit and be socially active.
2.	"The First Four Steps in Follow-up" Mock presentation of beginning follow-up (four steps)	Chapter 2	*Basic Bible Studies* Nos. 3 and 4	1 Cor. 10:13; John 6:47	Same as week No. 1
3.	"What Do Babies Need?" Discuss *Basic Bible Studies* No. 2.	Chapter 3	*Basic Bible Studies* No. 5	Ps. 119:11; John 16:24	Observe a follow-up visit and participate in the review of the Bible study.
4.	"The Adventure of a Follow-up Call" Mock presentation of a follow-up call	Chapter 4 Appendix A	*Basic Bible Studies* No. 6	1 Cor. 10:31; Matt. 4:19	Same as week No. 3
5.	"Equipping Saints for Follow-up" Discuss *Basic Bible Studies* No. 7.	Chapter 5 Appendix B	*Basic Bible Studies* No. 7	Eph. 5:18	Lead a follow-up visit with the trainer observing.
6.	"Beyond *Basic Bible Studies*" Discuss *Basic Bible Studies* No. 8	Chapter 6	*Basic Bible Studies* No. 8	Heb. 10:25	Same as week No. 5

The Pastor—a Shop Superintendent

Paul Lorenzen, in his excellent series on follow-up in the *Preacher's Magazine,* sets two objectives for us. He says:

Thus two comprehensive objectives can be clearly developed which will ultimately meet the needs of follow-up evangelism. The first objective may be stated as: to provide the love, nourishment, protection, and training necessary for the spiritual infant to grow into a spiritually mature Christian, faithfully serving Christ and the church under the leadership of the Holy Spirit.

The second objective may be stated as: to enable the spiritually mature (that is, older brothers and sisters in the family) to do the work of follow-up with the new Christians, providing the necessary parental care.[7]

For such goals to be achieved, we will need to consider the role of the pastor. He or she might be considered as a shop superintendent. The pastor does not do all the work but trains and coordinates the workers. As Eph. 4:11-12 puts it, "And He gave some . . . as evangelists, and some as pastors and teachers, for the equipping of the saints for the work of service, to the building up of the body of Christ" (NASB).

Waylon Moore says it is imperative that "the pastor . . . reemphasize in his own ministry the need of spending time with individuals, 'discipling men.'"[8] The central command of the Great Commission of Matt. 28:19-20 is to MAKE DISCIPLES. The other verbs in that commission are helping verbs— "going," "baptizing," and "teaching."[9]

Now a new tool is available to the pastor. *Basic Bible Studies* are so reasonably priced by Beacon Hill Press of Kansas City that it seems practical to provide such for every new convert. The tool for the beginning of his or her discipleship is here. Christians of longer duration will find their lives deepened as they begin their ministry of follow-up. Losses will diminish. The back door is shutting. The Church is growing and marching!—if, Pastor, you exercise your rightful ministry.

QUESTIONS FOR DISCUSSION

1. How would you differentiate between a spiritual parent and an adoptive spiritual parent?

2. What are some of the qualifications of an effective adoptive spiritual parent?

3. What are the responsibilities of the follow-up director?

4. How are adoptive spiritual parents chosen?

5. What place does training have in an effective follow-up ministry?

6. How would you describe the pastor's role of leadership in an effective follow-up program?

CHAPTER 6

Beyond *Basic Bible Studies*

OUR GOAL IS THE SAME AS PAUL'S: "We proclaim him, admonishing and teaching everyone with all wisdom, so that we may present everyone perfect in Christ" (Col. 1:28). Follow-up should enable believers to walk in the Spirit and live in spiritual victory (Rom. 8:4).

What Is a Mature Christian?

Waylon Moore says, "To disciple a man is to lead him to experience Jesus as Lord of all his life."[1] I have read and thought and tried to determine in my own mind what adequately defines a mature Christian. As I think of my yearnings for the growth of new Christians, I believe I have a definition. *A mature Christian is one who is able to stand alone under temptation, is able to spiritually reproduce, is involved in service for Christ, and is responsibly related to a local church.*

It is our hope that the attempt through *Basic Bible Studies* to get the new convert to begin reading systematically through John's Gospel (with some questions in each lesson on John) will result in enough discipline of life to prompt daily Scripture reading. The examples of personal application in *Basic Bible Studies* should help develop thought patterns that will enable the new Christian to find meaning in additional Bible reading beyond the verses in the eight lessons.

Filled with the Spirit

As conversion to Christ opened the door for the convert to begin Bible study, it is hoped that such study will lead him or her to a deeper experience with God. Lesson 7 is titled "Filled with God's Spirit." At the end of this study, there are four steps given for people to receive the fullness of the Spirit. The follow-up worker should expect to see times when spiritual children will pray right in their homes and be filled with the sanctifying Holy Spirit.

It has happened that way:

Tom and Joetta, in their late twenties, had never attended our church. We visited them because they had friends in our congregation. After hearing the gospel in their home one night, Tom and Joetta prayed and received Jesus into their lives. Immediately they were involved in the follow-up ministry. The change in their lives was quite evident. As they progressed through the eight Bible studies, they began to grow in the Lord. By Session 2, Joetta wanted to be baptized. By Session 4, both Tom and Joetta were witnessing to neighbors about the Lord. At Session 7, on sanctification, the follow-up worker asked if they wished to be filled with the Holy Spirit. Joetta said, "I beat you to it! I was sanctified this afternoon after doing the Bible study!" Tom said, "Yes," and they both knelt as Tom prayed and was filled with the Spirit in His sanctifying presence.

Tom and Joetta moved over 2,000 miles away, but now in their new church they have become active in the choir and are urging their new church to begin a lay-evangelism ministry. Joetta has been appointed director of the vacation Bible school.

Richard and Sharon, in their mid-thirties, both knelt that night in their home and, at the invitation of the visitors from our church, opened their hearts and lives to Jesus as Lord of their lives. The visitors immediately started them in the follow-up ministry by giving them Bible study No. 1. Over the course of the next 17 weeks, they completed the eight Bible studies and became active in the church. At Session 7, on sanctification, the worker invited them to pray for sanctification. Both of them knelt in their living room and dedicated themselves completely to God and received His Spirit in His fullness.

Their teen-age son has been saved, and Sharon is now public-relations representative in the evangelistic Bible correspondence school operated at the church. Both Richard and Sharon have become well established and are contributing members of the congregation.[2]

To be sanctified wholly by the filling of the Spirit is an establishing experience. The endurance powers of new Christians will be increased because of it.

Is the Convert Ready?

Sarah had found Christ one Sunday night after attending the evening service. She began Bible study and evidenced spiritual life. After about eight weeks, she had completed her studies, but then began to slip spiritually. She commented that she had done well while on the eight studies, but then . . . Could it be that we were not alert enough to our responsibilities **beyond** *Basic Bible Studies*?

It is readily admitted that most Christians are not adequately established in their faith after only eight Bible studies—and thus ready to stand alone under temptations. Usually, however, by the end of the eight studies, enough Christian friendships have been built by the new convert and enough other channels opened that there are other possibilities available to strengthen and maintain him or her.

At the completion of the *Basic Bible Studies,* an awards ceremony is held as part of the Sunday service, and the new Christian is presented a diploma[3] to mark his or her success. This public exposure encourages the convert by the public recognition and puts a reminder to show continued care in the hearts of the congregation.

Many converts ask for another Bible study series after completing *Basic Bible Studies;* and if they don't ask, they probably have the need. An excellent next step is to involve them in a group Bible study. Especially appropriate is the *Beacon Small-Group Bible Studies: The Gospel of John, Part One (Chapters 1—12)*[4] by Charles Shaver. This study should be aimed at continued establishment of the convert and at reaching his or her unsaved friends. A young Christian has friends in the world, but the longer one is a Christian, the more the Christian's friends will come from the church. The convert should be urged to invite these unsaved people to a group study while time and circumstances are right. After completion of *John, Part One,* the convert may be urged to do *John, Part Two*[5] by Shaver. Finally there is an intensive, high-commitment study titled *Living in the Power of the Spirit: A Discipleship Study—12 People Meeting for 12 Weeks for 12 Studies on the Work of the Spirit in the Life of the Believer,*[6] also by Shaver. This will lead believers into the experience of entire sanctification. Together *Basic Bible Studies,* the two John studies, and *Living in the Power of the Spirit* make up a one-year discipleship program in manageable segments that all Christians should be led through.

The John study works best in a home setting, and this group holds special values due to its dual emphasis on fellowship and the Word. If it is not possible to establish a group, the *John, Part One* study may be done on an individual basis or on a one-on-one basis.

If it is not possible to get an intensive discipleship group together, as in *Living in the Power of the Spirit,* there is an alternative. You may deepen the life of your new convert by leading him or her through another Bible study similar to *Basic Bible Studies.* It is *Basic Bible Studies for the Spirit-filled and Sanctified Life.*[7]

Usually by completion of *Basic Bible Studies,* the convert has become involved in a Sunday School class and the regular services of the church. These are normal channels for continued involvement and growth. Every contact with Christians means added strength. The follow-up worker bears some responsibility to introduce the convert to new people so this strength will be available.

A "church with enough love to keep them warm" is essential at this point. Fred and Patty, previously mentioned, after finding Christ, doing *Basic Bible Studies,* and joining the church, moved to a new city because of Fred's work. They were four and a half months old in the Lord at the time of the move—still pretty young. A shaky period seemed to be evident when their first visits to Nazarene churches did not seem to supply the warmth they needed.

Back at our local church that loved Fred and Patty, it was mentioned that they needed encouragement. It was suggested that members of the congregation could write a note to this couple on their Friendship in Worship cards[8] during the service. These cards were deposited in the offering plate at the time the offering was taken. The church office mailed over 30 encouraging notes to Fred and Patty that week. In addition they also received four personal letters. Then a long-distance phone call revealed they were "over the hump," praising the Lord, and getting involved in a local church.

The Continuing Touch

Perhaps the most important way to establish new converts beyond *Basic Bible Studies* is to make them part of a small group. This group will be dedicated to love, support, and caring. It will include accountability, which will mean the convert will be held responsible for growth. Also more mature Christians are responsible for the new Christian's growth. The previously mentioned sequence of *Basic Bible Studies, John I, John II,* and *Living in the Power of the Spirit* can meet this need for a year, but there are many small-group models available today that are effective. Many Christian leaders believe continued spiritual growth is possible only by continued involvement in a small group, perhaps even for life.

A Shift Toward Service

Dale and Sharon Carter are two Roman Catholics who have found Christ and discovered a spiritual home at our church. One Sunday they came up to me and said something like this: "You know, Pastor Shaver, we have been taking in so much from the Lord and having our needs so supplied here that it is time for us to begin to put out and do something more for the Lord." That kind of statement is a strong sign of maturity. The spiritual children are growing up. It would seem they are established.

Let me tell you one more story. It reveals the many factors that reach people for Christ and help hold them true. It shows a couple's growth as they are loved and followed up and the beginning of a shift from consumption and dependence to outreach and service. Here it is.

When I first came on the staff at First Church, I met Jan, a young wife and mother, who attended our services on Sunday mornings. One time I mentioned that I would like to meet her husband, who was not attending. Jan was fearful lest any call I might make would upset her husband.

A prayer letter went out to small-group leaders requesting prayer for our personal evangelism outreach. Ben Brown, Jan's Sunday School teacher, became burdened in prayer for Chuck, her husband, who seemed to be pulling farther away from Christ. Ben urged me to call on Chuck. On a March 17, Evelyn Smith, Allen Hall, and I went to call on Chuck and Jan. I was very fearful. It was a friendship call; we stayed only 20 minutes; we did not mention spiritual things; we only invited Chuck to church.

The next Sunday Chuck was in church. Then he came again. After one service I greeted him at the door and suggested I would like to stop by to see him again. On May 1, Tom

Bright, Laura Bowerman, and I called on Chuck and Jan. The Holy Spirit opened doors and hearts were prepared. Chuck and Jan prayed; Jesus came into their hearts; the assurance of heaven became theirs; and their lives were immediately made new. On the following Sunday they both knelt at First Church's altars as testimony of their commitment to Christ. Elmer Williams began to meet with them regularly to guide them as they began *Basic Bible Studies.*

A new sensitivity seemed to grip them. Chuck's language took on a new wholesomeness at work. Jan decided it would better glorify God if she refrained from attending the Hollywood movie she had planned to go to. God's love so engulfed them that Chuck said their marriage moved up to honeymoon status.

The small group in their area had not had a strong start, but Chuck and Jan volunteered their home for the first meeting, and 14 attended. They became aware of a member of their group who had transportation difficulties in getting to church. Chuck and Jan made a way possible for her. They had a loving concern to share Christ with their loved ones.

Chuck appeared at a seminary class and joyfully shared his faith in Christ. Sundays and Wednesdays you would find them worshiping at First Church. May 11, Chuck joined the church by profession of faith. Jan stood beside him and renewed her membership vows.

This one redeemed couple represents so much of what outreach means at First Church. There is prayer by many people, concerned Sunday School teachers, friendship calling, personal evangelism, the worship service, the altar, follow-up, small groups, and, most of all, the faithful work of the Holy Spirit.

May the Chucks and Jans of your area be reached and established. Yes, *conserve those converts.* If you do, today's spiritual babies will become tomorrow's spiritual parents. And Jesus Christ will have thousands more to serve and praise Him!

QUESTIONS FOR DISCUSSION

1. How would you answer the question "What is a mature Christian?"

2. What purposes might be accomplished by the public presentation of the diploma for the completion of the *Basic Bible Studies*?

3. How can group Bible study contribute to the continuing spiritual progress of the new Christian?

4. How will sharing their faith with others help to strengthen new Christians?

5. In what ways has this study helped you?

Appendix A

Records and Other Materials Used in Follow-up

(Items that may be ordered from Beacon Hill Press of Kansas City, Box 419527, Kansas City, MO 64141, 1-800-877-0700, are preceded by a star [★]. For convenience in ordering these items, an order number is listed. Items preceded by a check mark [✓] you may feel free to reproduce on your own Xerox.)

★ 1. Picture of Christ Knocking at the Door. (AW-250) Used as a Spiritual Birth Certificate

★ 2. *Basic Bible Studies for New/Growing Christians* (VE-80) is an item you should have with you while studying this book.

★ 3. "What Happened to Me?" (VE-81)

1 What Happened to Me?

Look up in your New Testament or Bible the answers to the following questions. When it says John 1:12, it means the Book of John, chapter 1, verse 12. (The index in the front of your New Testament or Bible will list the page number.) Read the answer from the Bible, then write it in your own words. In case you have only a New Testament, the Old Testament scriptures are written out in this study for you.

1. When I received Christ by personal invitation, I became a _____

   _____ of God (John 1:12).

2. The coming of Christ into the life or heart of an individual is a

   personal relationship between Christ and the one receiving Him,

   described by Christ in Revelation 3:20.

   a. Who is knocking at the door? (See Revelation 1:1 for further

      identification.) _____

   b. Who may answer His voice and knock? _____

      _____

   c. What does He want me to do? _____

      _____

   d. What will He do if I open the door? _____

      _____

✓ 4. Personal Evangelism Visit Results Form

PERSONAL EVANGELISM VISIT RESULTS FORM

Name of Prospect _____ Phone _____

Address _____ City _____

Date of Evangelistic Visit _____ Results _____
(Use code below)

Prospect's contact with Church of the Nazarene: ( )Attends regularly; ( ) Recently began attending; ( ) Has come on occasion; ( ) Visitor to recent service; ( ) Children attend Sunday School; ( ) Has been called on by (whom) _____; ( ) Has had positive contact with our laymen (whom) _____; ( ) Other, specify _____ ; Date last attended _____.

EVANGELISM TEAM _____

Who made the presentation? _____

Answer to first question _____

Answer to third question _____

Gospel presentation completed? Yes _____ No _____. Was profession made? Yes _____ No _____.

Attitude favorable or unfavorable _____.

(See next page for lower half of sheet.)

79

Profession only:

Name of person making profession _____

Appointment made for follow-up next day? Yes___ No___

Specific time_____ Other day _____ Date _____

Did you leave *Basic Bible Bible Study* No. 1? Yes___ No___

Does convert have a Bible or New Testament? Yes___ No___

Did you leave a New Testament with him or her? Yes___ No___

Did convert agree to make a public profession at church? Yes___ No___

When will this profession be? _____

Who will begin the follow-up? _____

Christian only:

Name of Christian_____

Is he or she a member of a church? Yes___ No___. Attends? Yes___ No___

What church? _____

Problems or comments: _____

_____

_____

PROF—Gospel presented, profession made
GPND—Gospel presented, no decision
REJ—Gospel presented, rejected
GPA—Gospel presented for assurance
XN—Already a Christian

TEST—Personal testimony only given
NH—No one at home
NO ADM—No admittance; would not let us in
FRV—Just a friendly visit
FOL UP—Made a follow-up call

✓ 5. Follow-up Session Summary

FOLLOW-UP SESSION SUMMARY

Name of Convert	Date Saved	Follow-up Worker	No. 1	No. 2	No. 3	No. 4	No. 5	No. 6	No. 7	No. 8	Small-Group Assign.

★ 6. *Now That I'm a Christian: Basic Bible Studies for Youth* (YD-501)

★ 7. *Now That I'm a Christian: Basic Bible Studies for Children* (VE-50)

★ 8. Friendship Registration Pad

FRIENDSHIP REGISTRATION PAD

(1) Record your name and check or enter other pertinent information
(2) Pass the pad to the next person

(3) When it reaches the end of the row pass it back, noting the names of others.
(4) After the benediction, greet your fellow-worshippers by name.

MEMBERS AND REGULAR ATTENDERS	GUESTS
Name _____ New Address _____ New Phone _____ New ZIP _____ ☐ Member ☐ Regular Attender	Name _____ Phone _____ Address _____ City/State _____ ZIP _____ No. in family _____ Invited by _____ ☐ 1st time visitor ☐ Return visitor ☐ Married ☐ Single ☐ Youth ☐ Child I regularly attend church at _____
Name _____ New Address _____ New Phone _____ New ZIP _____ ☐ Member ☐ Regular Attender	**I am interested in:** ☐ Accepting Christ as Savior ☐ Membership in this church ☐ Appointment with Pastor ☐ Special Prayer ☐ Locating a Sunday School class ☐ Home Bible Study ☐ Church offering envelopes ☐ A job in the church — **My (our) age:** ☐ Under 6 ☐ 6–11 ☐ 12–19 ☐ 20–30 ☐ 31–49 ☐ 50–65 ☐ Over 65 — **Age groups in family:** ☐ Under 6 ☐ 6–11 ☐ 12–19 ☐ 20–30 ☐ 31–49 ☐ 50–65 ☐ Over 65
Name _____ New Address _____ New Phone _____ New ZIP _____ ☐ Member ☐ Regular Attender	I heard about this church from: ☐ drove by ☐ media ☐ mailing ☐ other _____
Name _____ New Address _____ New Phone _____ New ZIP _____ ☐ Member ☐ Regular Attender	Name _____ Phone _____ Address _____ City/State _____ ZIP _____ No. in family _____ Invited by _____ ☐ 1st time visitor ☐ Return visitor ☐ Married ☐ Single ☐ Youth ☐ Child I regularly attend church at _____
Name _____ New Address _____ New Phone _____ New ZIP _____ ☐ Member ☐ Regular Attender	**I am interested in:** ☐ Accepting Christ as Savior ☐ Membership in this church ☐ Appointment with Pastor ☐ Special Prayer ☐ Locating a Sunday School class ☐ Home Bible Study ☐ Church offering envelopes ☐ A job in the church — **My (our) age:** ☐ Under 6 ☐ 6–11 ☐ 12–19 ☐ 20–30 ☐ 31–49 ☐ 50–65 ☐ Over 65 — **Age groups in family:** ☐ Under 6 ☐ 6–11 ☐ 12–19 ☐ 20–30 ☐ 31–49 ☐ 50–65 ☐ Over 65
Name _____ New Address _____ New Phone _____ New ZIP _____ ☐ Member ☐ Regular Attender	I heard about this church from: ☐ drove by ☐ media ☐ mailing ☐ other _____
Name _____ New Address _____ New Phone _____ New ZIP _____ ☐ Member ☐ Regular Attender	Name _____ Phone _____ Address _____ City/State _____ ZIP _____ No. in family _____ Invited by _____ ☐ 1st time visitor ☐ Return visitor ☐ Married ☐ Single ☐ Youth ☐ Child I regularly attend church at _____
Name _____ New Address _____ New Phone _____ New ZIP _____ ☐ Member ☐ Regular Attender	**I am interested in:** ☐ Accepting Christ as Savior ☐ Membership in this church ☐ Appointment with Pastor ☐ Special Prayer ☐ Locating a Sunday School class ☐ Home Bible Study ☐ Church offering envelopes ☐ A job in the church — **My (our) age:** ☐ Under 6 ☐ 6–11 ☐ 12–19 ☐ 20–30 ☐ 31–49 ☐ 50–65 ☐ Over 65 — **Age groups in family:** ☐ Under 6 ☐ 6–11 ☐ 12–19 ☐ 20–30 ☐ 31–49 ☐ 50–65 ☐ Over 65
	I heard about this church from: ☐ drove by ☐ media ☐ mailing ☐ other _____

Turn to the next sheet when this one is full. Last person in row please return pad to starting point.

✓ 9. Convert Follow-up Report Card or Convert Nurturing Report (VE-90)

CONVERT FOLLOW-UP REPORT CARD

NAME OF CONVERT_____ REPORT DATE_____
NAME OF FOLLOW-UP WORKER _____
 I. *Follow-up Bible Study Session*: Date of session_____
    (Circle the appropriate answer.)
    1. Bible study covered *(Basic Bible Study)* No. 1, No. 2, No. 3,
       No. 4, No. 5, No. 6, No. 7, No. 8.
    2. Contact was (enthusiastic, warm, cool, negative) at the visit.
    3. Grasp of subject covered last visit was (good, fair, poor).
    4. Response to material covered this visit was (good, fair, poor).
    5. Contact has (problems, no problems) with his or her deci-
       sion thus far.
    6. Contact (has, has not) promised to be in SS this Sunday.
    7. Contact (did, did not) have assurance of salvation when I left.
    8. I (have, have not) volunteered to bring him or her to church.
    9. Has your contact expressed an interest in some phase of the
       church program? (Yes, no.) If yes, what area?_____
 II. *Fellowship Contacts:* (Check the appropriate boxes.)
    ☐ Contact was in my home this week for social visit.
    ☐ I was in my contact's home for social visit.
    ☐ I talked with contact on the phone during the week about a
      problem. (List problem if possible.)_____
    ☐ Other _____
(Back)
III. *Recommendations:* (Check the appropriate boxes.)
    ☐ Pastor or staff member should make a home call.
    ☐ Personal evangelism team should call on other members of
      the contact's family. (Which family members in particular?)
      _____
    ☐ Teacher of Sunday School class should contact the new convert.
    ☐ There should be a change in follow-up personnel.
      Reason:_____
      _____
    ☐ Convert has been approached about baptism and/or member-
      ship at the conclusion of the study series. (Circle which one.)
    ☐ Convert has consented to baptism and/or membership. (Cir-
      cle one.)
    ☐ Other _____
IV. *Evaluation:* Write out any evaluation or comments you have con-
    cerning the convert. _____
    _____
    _____

Convert Nurturing Report

NAME OF CONVERT _____ DATE OF REPORT _____

NAME OF NURTURING WORKER _____
CIRCLE OR CHECK THE APPROPRIATE RESPONSES TO YOUR VISIT

I. **Basic Bible Study Session:** Date of session _____
  1. Bible study covered (Basic Bible Study 1, 2, 3, 4, 5, 6, 7, 8). Other _____
  2. Contact was enthusiastic, warm, cool, negative) at the visit.
  3. Grasp of subject covered last visit was (good, fair, poor).
  4. Response to material covered last visit was (good, fair, poor).
  5. Contact has (problems, no problems) with his decision thus far.
  6. Contact (did, did not) have assurance of salvation when I left.
  7. Contact (has, has not) promised to be in Sunday School this coming Sunday.
  8. I (have, have not) volunteered to bring him to church.
  9. Has your contact expressed an interest in some phase of the church program?

II. **Fellowship Contacts:**
  Contact was in my home this week for social visit.
  I was in my contact's home for social visit.
  I talked with contact on the phone during the week about a problem. (List th...
  Other _____

III. **Recommendations:**
  ☐ Pastor or staff member should make a home call.
  ☐ Personal evangelism team should call on other members of the contacts family. (Which family members in particular?).

  Teacher of Sunday School class should contact the new convert.
  ☐ There should be a change in nurturing personnel. (State reason _____

  ☐ Convert has been approached about baptism and/or membership at the conclusion of the study series (circle which one).
  ☐ Convert has consented to baptism and/or membership (circle which one).
  ☐ Other _____

IV. **Evaluation.** Write out any evaluation or comments you have concerning the convert.
_____
_____
_____
_____
_____

★ 10. This is a certificate folder awarded in recognition of those who complete *Basic Bible Studies* (VE-80). A certificate is included with each set of *Basic Bible Studies.*

Awarded to
_____
for completion of
Basic Bible Studies
❖
Church _____
Study Partner _____
Pastor _____
Date _____

CERTIFICATE
OF
RECOGNITION
❖

★ 11. *Basic Bible Studies for the Spirit-filled and Sanctified Life* (VE-91)

★ 12. Friendship in Worship Card (R-80)

(Front)

FRIENDSHIP IN WORSHIP

DATE _____

Number in Family _____

Mr.
Mrs.
NAME(s) Miss _____

PHONE _____

INVITED BY _____

ADDRESS _____ street

CITY _____ state _____ zip

MEMBER OF
THIS CHURCH ____

REGULAR
ATTENDANT ____

VISITOR ____

FIRST-TIME
VISITOR ____

SERVICE ATTENDING:
SS ____
WORSHIP a.m. ____
p.m. ____

I AM INTERESTED IN:
ACCEPTING CHRIST AS SAVIOUR ____
MEMBERSHIP IN THIS CHURCH ____
APPOINTMENT WITH PASTOR ____
SPECIAL PRAYER ____
LOCATING A SUNDAY SCHOOL
CLASS ____
A FELLOWSHIP GROUP ____
HOME BIBLE STUDY ____
CHURCH OFFERING ENVELOPES ____
A JOB IN THE CHURCH ____

**AGE GROUPS IN
MY FAMILY:**
Under 6 ____
6 - 11 ____
12 - 14 ____
15 - 17 ____
18 - 30 ____
31 - 40 ____
41 - 50 ____
51 - 60 ____
Over 60 ____

(Back)

INFORMATION

_____
_____
_____
_____
_____
_____
_____
_____
_____
_____

A B C D E F G H I J K L M
N O P Q R S T U V W X Y Z

R—80

Appendix B

Instructions for Use of
Basic Bible Studies for New/Growing Christians

The Bible studies and other materials mentioned in these instructions are designed to meet the basic needs of personal follow-up of the new Christian. To get the maximum benefit from the follow-up visits, it is suggested that the follow-up worker use the General and Special Instructions listed below as a guide. Everything mentioned will not need to be used with every new Christian, but wisdom should be exercised in omitting any material or disregarding any instructions.

Tailor your follow-up sessions to meet individual needs of your assigned new Christian, but do so prayerfully and carefully, changing the suggested procedure only when you are confident that the change will be beneficial. Remember that the training of the spiritual child must have the four basic essentials of (1) eating (the Word), (2) talking (prayer), (3) walking (obedience), and (4) sharing (witnessing).[1]

General Instructions

The following general instructions should be observed for each follow-up session you have with your new Christian. Review them before each session.

I. PREPARATION FOR THE SESSION
   A. Pray before you arrive at the home of the new Christian. Be sure that you are up-to-date in your own spiritual life.
   B. Read the Special Instructions for the session you are about to have with your new Christian. Know what you are going to be doing *before you arrive.*

C. Be prompt and cheerful. You are doing God's work; *Do It Well!*

D. Most of all—*Be Consistent!*

II. INSTRUCTIONS FOR THE SESSION

A. Begin each follow-up session with a social visit. Use this time to reestablish rapport with the new Christian, and move into the Bible study when the atmosphere seems appropriate to do so.

B. The following 10 items are taken from *Follow-up Made Easy* by C. S. Lovett.[2]

1. *Don't get off the subject.* Stay on target. Be objective in your discussions. Point to Christ. Don't use precious time to ventilate your personal feelings.

2. *Watch the time.* Don't impose. Keep your eyes on the clock. Be selective in dealing with questions. Don't get bogged down and use teaching time on unrelated things.

3. *Don't teach too fast.* A baby feeds from a bottle, not a fire hose.

4. *Don't give him [or her] too much.* Regardless of whether your new Christian seems to be a ready listener, refrain from giving too much at a time.

5. *Avoid controversial questions.* It has been well said that the mind of man can ask questions the mind of man can't answer, and that the answer may not be recognized by either questioner or answerer (Dr. Gutzke, Columbia Seminary). Stay with the fundamentals of the faith. . . . "The wayfaring men, though fools, shall not err therein" (Isa. 35:8, KJV).

6. *Don't go unprepared.* "Study to shew thyself approved unto God, a workman that needeth not to be ashamed, rightly dividing the word of truth" (2 Tim. 2:15, KJV).

7. *Watch bad breath.* 'Nuff said!

8. *Don't bring gloom into the convert's home.* Lay your burdens on the Lord and ask Him to fill you with the fruit of the Spirit (Gal. 5:22-23).

9. *Don't teach with a know-it-all attitude.* Be positive in your teaching, not wishy-washy, maybe-so; but watch your attitude. State your earnest convictions to yourself in front of a mirror, and watch your expressions. You'll be glad you did.

10. *Don't argue.* See 2 Timothy 2 for help on this point.

C. Be sure to include a time of prayer during the call. Probably the best time will be following the Bible study. Ask the new Christian if he or she has any special needs that you should pray for, and pray especially for these. As soon as the new Christian is able, have that one join you in praying verbally, not just silently (but do not force this issue).

D. Set or confirm the time of your next meeting with your new Christian. Be sure that the time is still convenient for both of you. Write down the time so that neither of you forgets this appointment.

E. Urge the new Christian to attend Sunday School and church each Sunday. Offer to pick him or her up with your car if this is necessary to get attendance. At any time during the follow-up effort, should the new Christian seem to experience spiritual failure, you may quite naturally lead into a discussion of his or her need by reviewing the five ways to grow spiritually on the back of lesson No. 1.

III. INSTRUCTIONS FOR FOLLOWING THE SESSION

A. Fill out the Report Card as fully as you can. Do not worry about duplicating information you have reported before. Make any suggestions you may have that you think may help either your new Christian or the follow-up program as a whole.

B. Return the completed Report Card to the properly designated person as soon as possible (at least by the next time you are at church). Be sure that you are up-to-date on communicating with your Report Cards. This line of communication is vital to the success of the total ministry of follow-up.

C. Be sure your new Christian is on your prayer list. Pray for him or her during your own quiet time.

Special Instructions

The following instructions are for the worker's use with each individual Bible study in the set of eight lessons. Each set of instructions should be read *before* the worker arrives at the home of the new Christian. Notes should be taken from the instruction sheet and these notes used to plan the session of study. Usually only the material for a particular session should be taken to the new Christian's home; the rest of the material should be left in the packet at home.

The worker should try to read at least one week ahead in the instructions so that he or she will have materials together before the session and will know what to expect well in advance.

Lesson No. 1: *What Happened to Me?*

I. TESTING THE NEW CHRISTIAN'S ASSURANCE OF SALVATION

The first follow-up visit is the time to nail down the understanding of what has happened in his or her life. *You know* what the "new babe" should understand, but *your* idea of what happened and *the convert's* idea may be altogether different. Use a question or two from the following selection to ascertain the assurance and understanding of the convert:

- "Do you know if you have eternal life?"
- "If you were to die tonight in your sleep, where would you wake up?"

- "Why should God let you into His heaven?"
- "———, if someone were to ask you how to become a Christian, what would you say?"

II. WORKING THROUGH THE BIBLE STUDY

Whether your new Christian was converted at the altar, through mass evangelism, or in the home through personal evangelism, he or she will have received a copy of *Basic Bible Study* No. 1, "What Happened to Me?" When the atmosphere seems comfortable, bring up the subject of this Bible study, and begin working with the new Christian on it.

A. Go over lesson No. 1 with the new Christian. If the convert hasn't done the lesson, help with several answers and reassign or go through the whole lesson with him or her. *Pay special attention to questions Nos. 13 and 14.* This is the primary goal of this first session—to be sure of the new Christian's assurance of eternal life and forgiveness of his or her sins.

B. Write down any questions that you can't answer, and find out the answer before the next session.

C. If the new Christian does not already have one, give a Spiritual Birth Certificate—use the picture of Jesus standing at the door knocking. Point out that (1) the light behind Jesus forms the shape of a heart, and (2) there is no latch on the door; it must be opened from the inside. This picture illustrates Rev. 3:20. When the new Christian opened his or her heart to Jesus as Lord and Savior, Jesus came into that heart. Write on the back of the picture as illustrated on the next page:

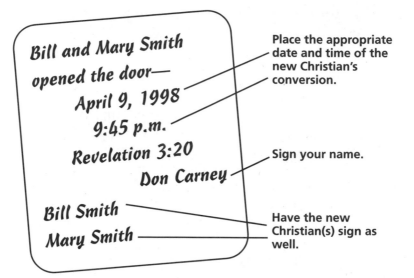

Bill and Mary Smith
opened the door—
April 9, 1998
9:45 p.m.
Revelation 3:20
Don Carney

Bill Smith
Mary Smith

Place the appropriate date and time of the new Christian's conversion.

Sign your name.

Have the new Christian(s) sign as well.

Give this Birth Certificate to the new Christian to keep as a personal record of when he or she was born again.

D. Give the new Christian a copy of some appropriate literature introducing your local church.

E. Quiz him or her on the memory verse (Rev. 3:20), and go over the five ways to grow spiritually on the back of lesson No. 1.

III. GIVING THE ASSIGNMENT FOR NEXT SESSION

Important: Never Give an Assignment That You Don't Intend to Follow through on at the Next Session!

A. Assign the first two chapters of the Gospel of John for the new Christian's reading for the coming week. Stress the importance of Bible reading in the life of the Christian.

B. Give the new Christian lesson No. 2, "Walking with God," and point out the memory verse (1 Cor. 10:13) to learn.

C. Encourage the convert to work through the lesson on his or her own before your next session with him or her.

D. Give the colored packet to store his or her completed studies in. On this packet write your name and phone number.

Lesson No. 2: *Walking with God*

The primary purpose of this lesson is to give the new Christian the needed weapons to be able to effectively combat Satan and the temptations that he or she is sure to encounter. Do everything you can *To Encourage* the new Christian this session!

Be sure you reviewed the General Instructions!

I. REVIEW

Briefly review the material covered during the last session. Be sure the convert still has assurance of salvation before continuing with lesson No. 2.

II. LESSON TWO
A. Go over the questions he or she has been able to answer in lesson No. 2, and help answer any that are incomplete.
1. Questions Nos. 9 and 11 are the key questions to this study.
2. Use the blank space on the back of lesson No. 3, which you have brought with you to leave with the new Christian, to draw the "train illustration" shown on the next page. You may want to share 1 Pet. 1:8 and then say something like: "The train will run with or without the caboose. However, it would be futile to attempt to pull the train by the caboose. In the same way, we as Christians do not depend on feelings or emotions, but place our faith (trust) in the trustworthiness of God and the promises of His Word."[3]
B. Quiz on the memory verse (1 Cor. 10:13).

III. ASSIGNMENT FOR NEXT SESSION
  A. Assign the third and fourth chapters of the Gospel of John. Continue to stress the importance of Bible reading in the life of the Christian.
  B. Give the new Christian lesson No. 3, and point out the memory verse (Ps. 119:11) to start learning.
  C. Encourage the convert to work through lesson No. 3 on his or her own before your next session together.

Lesson No. 3: *Learning from God*

The purpose of this lesson is to give the new Christian a foundation in the reasons for and results of Bible study. **Suggestion:** If it hasn't already been done, you might obtain a copy of some inexpensive modern translation of the New Testament to give to the new Christian. It is much easier to understand the Bible in the modern-language translations and paraphrases.

  I. REVIEW
Briefly review the material covered during the last session. Ask the new convert to share with you any victories experienced over temptation this last week.

 II. LESSON THREE
  A. Go over the questions he or she has been able to answer in lesson No. 3, and help answer any that are incomplete.
  B. Question No. 11 should express his or her own thinking. Encourage a full answer.
  C. Quiz on the memory verse (Ps. 119:11).

III. ASSIGNMENT FOR NEXT SESSION
   A. Assign the fifth and sixth chapters of the Gospel of John.
   B. Give lesson No. 4, and point out the memory verse (John 16:24) to start learning.
   C. Again, encourage the convert to begin working through lesson No. 4 on his or her own.

Lesson No. 4: *Talking with God*

The purpose of this lesson is to encourage the new Christian to establish the habit of daily prayer. **Suggestion:** Share with the new Christian some of the joys and experiences you have had as a result of a regular devotional time each day.

   I. REVIEW
   Briefly review the material covered during the last session. Ask the new Christian to share some of the discoveries he or she made during the last week reading the fifth and sixth chapters of John's Gospel.

   II. LESSON FOUR
   A. Go over the questions he or she has been able to answer in lesson No. 4, and help answer any that are incomplete. Discuss the answer to No. 11.
   B. Urge the new Christian to list prayer requests on the back of lesson No. 4 and refer to this list during his or her quiet time this coming week.
   C. Quiz on the memory verse (John 16:24).

   III. ASSIGNMENT FOR NEXT SESSION
   A. Assign the seventh and eighth chapters of the Gospel of John.
   B. Give the new Christian lesson No. 5, and highlight the memory verse.
   C. Encourage working through it on his or her own.

IV. OPTIONAL

At the end of this session, begin to discuss the subject's obedience to the command to be baptized (Acts 2:38; 8:12) at the culmination of the series of eight lessons. Ask the convert to begin thinking about being baptized.

Lesson No. 5: *Sharing with God*

The purpose of this lesson is to encourage the new Christian to become a good steward of his or her entire life (money, time, energies, talents, etc.), reflecting the love of God through his or her behavior and pattern of living. Stewardship, though commonly related to giving of money, should be thought of as including all of the Christian's being.

I. REVIEW

Briefly review the material covered during the last session. Ask the new Christian to share the prayer list with you.

II. LESSON FIVE
  A. Go over the questions he or she has been able to answer in lesson No. 5, and help answer any that are incomplete.
  B. Discuss the memory verse for this week (1 Cor. 10:31) and its relation to question No. 9. Discuss several possible answers the new Christian might give for question No. 9.
  C. Share with the new Christian the concept that the life of the mature Christian is the way of expressing gratitude for God's love and His plan of salvation. "My LIFE says THANK YOU, God."
  D. Quiz on the memory verse (1 Cor. 10:31).

III. ASSIGNMENT FOR NEXT SESSION
  A. Assign the ninth and tenth chapters of the Gospel of John.
  B. Give the new Christian lesson No. 6, and direct him or her to the memory verse.

C. Encourage working through it on his or her own.

Lesson No. 6: *Speaking for God*

The purpose of this lesson is to encourage the new Christian to establish the habit of witnessing to friends and relatives whenever there is the opportunity. **Suggestion:** Share with the convert some experiences you have had witnessing about what Jesus has done for you. Let him know that witnessing should be the *rule* and *not the exception* among Christians.

I. REVIEW

Briefly review the material covered during the last session. Ask the new Christian the ways discovered to say "thank You" to God through the stewardship of life.

II. LESSON SIX
   A. Go over the questions he or she has been able to answer in lesson No. 6, and help answer any that are incomplete.
   B. Give him or her the *Life Can Have True Meaning* booklet,[+] and *read through it with the new Christian.* Encourage him or her to become familiar with the contents in order to share Christ with others by means of this booklet.
   C. Quiz on the memory verse (Matt. 4:19).

III. ASSIGNMENT FOR NEXT SESSION
   A. Assign the eleventh and twelfth chapters of the Gospel of John.
   B. Give the new Christian lesson No. 7, and show the memory verse.
   C. Encourage working through it on his or her own.

IV. OPTIONAL
   A. Question the new Christian again concerning the subject of baptism.

B. Set up a time with the convert when the two of you would visit a friend or relative of his or hers and witness, using the *Life Can Have True Meaning* booklet.

Lesson No. 7: *Filled with God's Spirit*

The purpose of this lesson is to prepare the new Christian for (and perhaps lead into) the filling and cleansing of the Holy Spirit in the experience of entire sanctification. **Suggestion:** Share with the new Christian your own experience of entire sanctification and how you have been able to be a more victorious Christian because of the fullness of the Holy Spirit in your life.

I. REVIEW

Briefly review the material covered during the last session. Ask the new Christian to share any experiences of witnessing during the last week. Encourage continued witnessing whenever there is the opportunity.

II. LESSON SEVEN

A. Go over the questions he or she has been able to answer in lesson No. 7, and help answer any that are incomplete.

B. Help the new Christian discover items in life that would need to be surrendered in order for him or her to be completely committed to Christ. Urge openness to the Spirit's prodding. Emphasize the four steps to be filled with the Spirit at the end of the study. Pray with the convert if he or she is already prepared for entire sanctification. (Be sure to make a notation on the weekly Report Card about what happens at this point. This communication is imperative.)

C. Give the new Christian a copy of the booklet *My Heart, Christ's Home,* by Robert Boyd Munger.[5] Urge prayerful reading of the booklet during the next week.

IV. OPTIONAL
   A. Attempt to arrive at a definite decision concerning baptism of the new Christian at the completion of the series of Bible studies.
   B. *Either:* Approach the new Christian about starting a Bible study in a home to which he or she would invite unsaved friends (John, Part One).
      Or: Approach the new Christian about joining a small Bible study when finished with the individual Bible studies.

Lesson No. 8: *Uniting for God*

The purpose of this lesson is to prepare the new Christian for church participation and membership. **Suggestion:** Share with the new Christian how much the church has meant to you and how much you benefit from participation in the activities of the local church.

I. REVIEW
   Briefly review the material covered during the last session.

II. LESSON EIGHT
   A. Go over the questions answered in lesson No. 8, and help answer any that are incomplete.
   B. Discuss with the convert the relationship of the church organization to the spiritual Body of Christ. (Note that one is a member of the Body of Christ from the moment of his or her new birth, but becoming a member of the local congregation of a church or denomination is a move made later and about which one must make a personal decision.)
   C. Quiz on the memory verse (Heb. 10:25).
   D. Give the new Christian a copy of the local church directory if one is available for your church.
   E. Ask the new Christian if you may give his or her name to the pastor as one interested in church membership.

III. TERMINATION OF THE LESSON SERIES
   A. Review the five ways to spiritual growth on the back of study No. 1, and help the new Christian evaluate personal spiritual progress according to the five areas mentioned. Circle the areas in which the most work is needed.
   B. Attempt to establish finally whether the convert will be baptized soon. (Set a date with the pastor before this session.)
   C. Discuss the home Bible study mentioned last week, and arrange with the follow-up coordinator for the study to begin;
   D. Or, make an appointment with the new Christian to take him or her to an established small-group Bible study already in progress.

ADDITIONAL NOTE:

When you have completed the full series of studies and your new Christian has become involved in further group Bible study, return any unused material from the packet to the follow-up coordinator.

Notes

DEFINITIONS:

1. Waylon Moore, *New Testament Follow-up for Pastors and Laymen* (Grand Rapids: William B. Eerdmans Publishing Co., 1973), 11.

CHAPTER 1:

1. The names of most individuals who were followed up or who followed up will be changed in the book to protect their privacy. The case histories are true.

2. C. E. Autrey, as quoted by Moore, *New Testament Follow-up,* 19.

3. A. C. Archibald, ibid., 99.

4. Fletcher Spruce, "Where Have They Gone?" (Paper presented at the Conference of Superintendents, Church of the Nazarene, at Kansas City, Jan. 23, 1975), 4.

5. Dawson Trotman, *Born to Reproduce,* Tape No. 2 (Phoenix: Inspirational Tape Ministries), makes this emphasis.

6. Paul Lorenzen, "Follow-up Evangelism, Part 1, Background," *Preacher's Magazine* 49, No. 8 (Aug. 1974): 15.

7. Walter Henrichsen, *Disciples Are Made—Not Born* (Wheaton, Ill.: Victor Books, 1974), 80.

8. Trotman, *Born to Reproduce.*

9. Paul Lorenzen, "Follow-up Evangelism, Part 6, The Results," *Preacher's Magazine* 50, No. 1 (Jan. 1975): 19. We must remember that in the study done by Fletcher Spruce, as noted above, over 54 percent are lost of those who have joined the church. This does not take into account a larger number who experience conversion, fall away, and have never joined the church. Sometime run a check on your congregation's first-time seekers for salva-

tion in a given year as compared to the number who join by profession of faith in that year.

CHAPTER 2:

1. Notice the relation of "repentance" and "opening the door" by comparing Rev. 3:19 with verse 20.

2. This picture may be ordered from the Beacon Hill Press of Kansas City. See Appendix A, item 1, for further details.

3. There are times when you may need to ask the new converts to give verbal testimony of their newfound relationship with Christ instead of coming to the altar. I did this with a 66-year-old woman who found Christ for the first time in her life on a Tuesday night. Since the very next service was Wednesday prayer meeting and a testimony time would be included in that, it was natural to ask that lady to give her testimony then. She did so joyously the next night. You must decide what you think will be best for your convert in his or her particular situation.

4. Charles "Chic" Shaver, *Basic Bible Studies for New/ Growing Christians,* 2nd ed. (Kansas City: Beacon Hill Press of Kansas City, 1994). See Appendix A, item 2, for further details.

5. See Appendix A, item 3.

6. See Appendix A, item 4.

7. See Appendix A, item 5.

8. Published in *First Church of the Nazarene in Focus,* Kansas City (Apr. 3, 1975). This is the church's weekly newsletter.

CHAPTER 3:

1. Moore, *New Testament Follow-up,* 24.

2. Ibid., 27.

3. Ibid., 33.

4. This record-keeping material will be discussed more at length later in this book.

5. Mark Gilroy, ed., *Now That I'm a Christian: Basic Bible Studies for Youth* (Kansas City: Beacon Hill Press of Kansas

City, 1991). These are adapted from *Basic Bible Studies* by Charles "Chic" Shaver. See Appendix A, item 6.

6. Donna Fillmore, *Now That I'm a Christian: Basic Bible Studies for Children* (Kansas City: Beacon Hill Press of Kansas City, 1996). See Appendix A, item 7.

7. Coral Ridge Presbyterian Church, Fort Lauderdale, Florida. Lecture of Dr. D. James Kennedy, Feb. 4, 1970.

8. See Appendix A, item 8.

9. This program has been used at First Church of the Nazarene, Kansas City.

10. Moore, *New Testament Follow-up,* 18.

CHAPTER 4:
1. See Appendix B.

CHAPTER 5:
1. Nazarene Theological Seminary, lecture of Dr. Howard Hendricks, "The Anatomy of Leadership," Oct. 8, 1974.

2. Moore, *New Testament Follow-up,* 103.

3. Refer to *Basic Bible Studies* to better understand the Record of Progress on this packet.

4. See Appendix A, item 9.

5. See Appendix A, item 5.

6. To be explained in more detail later.

7. Paul Lorenzen, "Follow-up Evangelism, Part 4, Its Objectives," *Preacher's Magazine* 49, No. 11 (Nov. 1974): 15.

8. Moore, *New Testament Follow-up,* 12.

9. Vergil Gerber, *A Manual for Evangelism/Church Growth* (Pasadena, Calif.: William Carey Library, 1973), 14.

CHAPTER 6:
1. Moore, *New Testament Follow-up,* 30.

2. Lorenzen, "Follow-up Evangelism, Part 6, The Results," 18-19.

3. See sample of diploma in Appendix A, item 10.

4. These are available from Beacon Hill Press of Kansas City.

5. Available through Beacon Hill Press of Kansas City.

6. Available through Beacon Hill Press of Kansas City.

7. Charles "Chic" Shaver, *Basic Bible Studies for the Spirit-filled and Sanctified Life* (Kansas City: Beacon Hill Press of Kansas City, 1991). See Appendix A, item 11.

8. See sample in Appendix A, item 12.

APPENDIX B:

1. Moore, *New Testament Follow-up*, 45.

2. C. S. Lovett, *Follow-up Made Easy*, 46-49.

3. Campus Crusade for Christ, *Have You Heard of the Four Spiritual Laws?* 12.

4. *Life Can Have True Meaning* booklet, published by Beacon Hill Press of Kansas City (VE-24B).

5. Robert Boyd Munger, *My Heart, Christ's Home* (Chicago: Inter-Varsity Christian Fellowship, 1967). This is available through Beacon Hill Press of Kansas City (BLS -113).